*Francis Ledwidge*

───────── ◆ ─────────

# Francis Ledwidge

◆

## Song of the Blackbird

### Elizabeth Cassidy Olson

**Writers Club Press**
San Jose  New York  Lincoln  Shanghai

Francis Ledwidge
Song of the Blackbird

All Rights Reserved © 2000 by Elizabeth Cassidy Olson

No part of this book may be reproduced or transmitted in any form or by any means, graphic, electronic, or mechanical, including photocopying, recording, taping, or by any information storage retrieval system, without the permission in writing from the publisher.

Writers Club Press
an imprint of iUniverse.com, Inc.

For information address:
iUniverse.com, Inc.
5220 S 16th, Ste. 200
Lincoln, NE 68512
www.iuniverse.com

ISBN: 0-595-14360-1

Printed in the United States of America

The morning haze hovered as a cloak over the Slane meadows. The white washed cottage with its newly thatched roof rested comfortably upon farm land that rose gently towards the Wicklow mountains which served as fences against the winds that swept across the valley of southwest Ireland.

Patrick Ledwidge, a gaunt weathered farmer, had lived here all of his sixty years. He knew well the contour of each hedgerow that marked his land. Each of his acres, ten in all, had shaped his lean frame. His large hands, with thick fingers, had built the cottage, barn and shed. The heavily lined face had looked upon dawns and twilights in this place since his birth. He knew each rise and fall of the dirt road which passed his cottage gate and led to the stone fountain in the center of Slane village from which both farmer, horse and sheep drank at the end of all trips from farm to the village on Fair Days.

This gentle spring morning Patrick Ledwidge, widower, turned his gaze towards the cottage focusing his attention on the upstairs window behind which his only son slept. The boy was lying on the trestled bed, arms under his blonde head. Young Francis Ledwidge, his widely spaced blue eyes now fully opened, concentrated upon the morning star which seemed to be resting upon the roof of the adjacent shed.

His lips moved and he half whispered those joyous words he had so longed to say today "Fair Day" he smiled broadly and repeated "Fair Day" at last!

Rising quickly he pulled on his trousers and put on the jacket which had carefully been brushed and lain on the chair near the window the evening before.

His hand quickly splashed the cool water in the basin over his face. He made little effort to clean that face upon which dreams had been recently interrupted.

He was putting on his socks when he heard a light brushing of wings against the window. Turning quickly he drew in his breath sharply.

A black bird stared back at him. It cocked its small head from side to side; its tiny eyes wide and unblinking.

"What can I do for you this fine morning?" Francis asked softly still sitting quietly, afraid his guest would depart.

His fears were realized. The bird lifted its wings and rose quickly into the wind. Francis followed its flight until it disappeared into the morning mist. Francis, seeing his father below waved excitedly.

The father lifted his head to his son and smiled. "Forgot your chores this morning have you my son?" "Not at all Da, it's still early, I've been thinking about my plan for the day."

"I think," the father accented, "**think**" WITH A LONG PAUSE.

"Don't worry Da, everything will be done just the way you told me, I'll go down and pour your tea now."

In the kitchen Francis poked the peat beneath the steaming pot on the hob speaking quickly to himself, "Fair Day at last, a whole day to myself – the chores won't take me long."

He placed the thick brown gruel into each bowl from the pan, then hurried back to the shelf for the two cups for tea.

The front door opened and his father entered. " A warm day already it is Francis." "Indeed it is father, no better day for selling your fine flock in town I'd say."

They ate in silence each to his own thoughts. Francis lifted his eyes to his father. "Da, I know you'll be selling all of them, I'm thinking —there will be twelve pounds in your pocket when you return."

Patrick put his cup down and smiled. "You exaggerate my boy, if I make five pounds on the lot, I'd consider it a more than decent return."

Francis rose and put the bowls and cups into the basin. His father took his black thorn stick from the hook by the door and went out to lead his sheep to the market place in Slane. Fair Day at last!

A few minutes passed until the boy heard the sheep bells fill the soft summer morning. His father paused at the gate—"Now, my son I depend on you this day to tend things as always—duty my boy is a noble endeavor; it forms the character."

"Yes, Da. I wish you a good day at the Fair".

Patrick smiled then led his sheep down the dirt road but before he turned the sheep towards town, he stopped and raised his black thorn stick in farewell.

A minute later Francis with a half-run bounded into the cottage and went directly to the shelf where the Bible and a few books were kept. Mr. Madden, the school master at the National School, had given him these treasures.

He reached for his favorite book titled *Brian Boru—Soldier and Poet—First Druid convert to Christianity*.

Out the door the boy went with his father's words echoing in his ears —"Duty my boy is a noble endeavor fading with each hurried step."

He jumped over several steps, then gaining momentum crossed the fields clutching tightly to the book, eager to reach his sanctuary—a small promontory near the mountain. Francis had named his place Ballynock. Here he became the hero of Irish folklore, Brian Boru. Here he would rule over his kingdom and command his noble soldier-army.

In this solitary place, with the Wicklow Mountains behind him and the meadows reaching to a distant horizon he was Brian Boru himself.

Upon reaching Ballynock he found his favorite rock, opened his book and forgot duty, replacing it with day-dreaming of battles to be fought and glory to be captured.

The sun crossed the heavens in its daily course, birds chatted and flew above Francis, unconcerned about the battles being fought so valiantly by the boy dreamer.

A distant chime intruded upon the silence of this sacred place.

Cow bells familiar at day's end to farmers filled the twilight as cattle moved towards their home pastures.

The boy awoke with a start. He jumped to his feet, the book falling from his hands. He saw that the sun had almost gone from the sky.

Mouth dry and tears welling into his eyes, he grasped the fallen book and ran towards home, no longer the hero but only Francis, son of Patrick, sure only of his disgrace.

As he ran he thought that some magic potion must have been given him by the little folk and left him senseless—a whole day!

Jumping over a stile he wondered how he could explain his neglect of duty to his father.

The fire that would be now out, the barn not swept, the cows not milked, the lamps not cleaned. He stopped for a moment and thought of running away—but where to go. He would sooner or later have to face his father. He walked with shoulders slumped in despair, the hero—no longer!

Patrick Ledwidge hurried in the late afternoon twilight towards home. In his pocket coins danced merrily, the sound brought a smile to his usually glum face.

"The boy was close to the truth when he said I'd get ten pounds for the sheep. Imagine nine pounds. I'm a rich man!" He laughed turning to see if anyone was about.

He had the road to himself.

The twilight lit the sky with plumes of pink and silver clouds. Patrick walked quickly eager to tell his son of his success.

He turned down the lane to the cottage and stopped abruptly.

No smoke from the chimney. A chill shook his being.

Moving slowly forward, he pushed open the gate, then the cottage door—empty—the fire dead.

Patrick slumped into the chair near the window. Ghosts walked before him, his wife and two children had come to tell him that the last son would join them in St. Brendan's graveyard.

He shook his head to clear his mind—he moaned aloud "Where is the boy?"—he stood, opened the door and walked to the barn and shed calling "Francis—Francis"—silence.

Francis thinking that maybe fate would save him yet prayed that Patrick might have lingered at the Fair longer and could be talking with the farmers later than expected.

He began to run. He leaped over ditches and bracken. The blood pounding in his temples—his brain searching for an excuse for his neglect of duty. Darkness came suddenly and closed out the day. The darkness caused the boy to lose his footing over once familiar rocks. He raced across a pond knee deep knowing he'd never find the grey flat stones which had earlier transported him toward his fortress at Ballynock.

The clock on the fireplace mantle ticked solemnly, then struck the hour.

Patrick rocked back and forth in the chair searching to find a reason for the boy's absence. He made his mind up to seek help. The nearest farm lay to the north a mile in distance. He knew he had to do something.

As he stood up he heard the running steps. The door opened and in the shaft of moonlight stood his son.

Before he could clasp the boy to himself, the boy's gasping words filled the small room.

"The tinkers got me Da, I was in the stable about to do me chores when one of them, sleeping in the loft he was, grabbed my arms—me screeching and hollering." Then, after more gasping and tears the narrative continued. Patrick listening attentively.

"They were going to the Fair, Da. They were looking for livestock, a stray pig, some hens—you know what thieves and blaggards they are Da."

The boy took a deep breath. "They started fighting as to who would take the livestock to the Fair. One said it was fool-hardy to bring the animals to the place, where all the farmers would be. They'd be knowing their own stock wouldn't they?"—Patrick remained silent during this remarkable tale wondering how it all would conclude.

"They decided there and then to take me back over the fields towards Navan Da and leave me by the bridge, knowing it would take me a good part of the day to get back home. They're scheming devils—just as you told me Da."

The tale continued.

"It got to be long past three o'clock before we got to the bridge."

Patrick cleared his throat.

"That will be enough, my son."

Francis dropped the book he had forgotten he had been clutching, so intent was he with his story.

He bent down to pick it up but Patrick saw it all too clearly now -

He kicked the slim volume of *Brian Boru—Soldier and Poet* into the hearth. Within minutes the kindling was lit and the peat crackled. Patrick moved to the shelf where the remaining books stood—taking all but the Bible, fearing God's Hand in the anger that now possessed him, he threw the lot into the fire.

Francis stared into the flames.

"Liar!" Patrick spat out the word lashing the boy in a way that the stick could never have accomplished.

"My own son—reading up there on his mountain—filling his mind with dreams. Leaving the house to spend a day—to waste a day I should say—doing little of anything but imagining himself to be someone he can never be—Brian Boru it is. He's been in his grave for many a year, my boy."

Francis, his mouth fighting to control his sobs turned and went up the stairs.

He closed his door softly and lay down turning his face into the pillow to keep the sobbing from his father's ears.

That night would be the end of Francis' childhood. His own father with his words of ridicule had torn away that secret place wherein he Francis Ledwidge had found courage, beauty and truth.

It was back to the shovel, the callused hands, the day-by-day routines which would stretch into a lifetime of servitude until the grave.

The black bird suddenly returned to his thoughts before he fell asleep. He remembered the bird with its wings opening wide, then it swept into flight and escaped!

Fair Day was never spoken of again, yet it lay each day in the hearts of Patrick and Francis like a living thing that made night and day no different.

Indeed the blackbird had been a harbinger of change. Francis remembered it as he put his head upon the pillow in that quiet house each night. The last thing he would see were its black wings open and ready for flight.

The National School was a distance of three miles from the Ledwidge cottage. Francis was permitted to attend only if his father agreed that he was not needed at home. There in the classroom with its long refractory desks, and small wooden stools, Francis knew the power and joy of sharing the unknown. He wrote on his tablet the many dreams he had stored for so long in his mind. The master, Mr. Madden, a kind and gentle man not yet thirty years of age, gave his charges the best of himself. His ruddy cheeks and jovial manner brought laughter into Francis' life—something he knew little about!

One day in early April, when the hawthorn bushes were swelling into renewed bloom and the fields were carpeted with green, Francis found himself in the stable putting down new hay. His father had promised he could attend school the following day if the chores assigned had been completed. He moved quickly—laying the hay, cleaning the lanterns, and filling them with kerosene. As the sky darkened, he knew he must hurry to start the supper. No thought but to please his father and gain permission to return to class was on his mind.

As he entered the kitchen door, he heard voices, familiar voices, in the unused parlor. It was his father and the schoolmaster in heated conversation. The kitchen door was latched so Francis moved closer to the wall to catch the words being spoken.

"You see, Mr. Ledwidge, it is imperative that Francis attend school regularly. He is a gifted student, far best than any I've taught. With discipline and opportunity I believe he will someday become a poet." The master's voice was strong with conviction. He stopped and waited for Patrick's response. Hearing none he plunged on. "This boy of yours sir, should apply for the new term at the Priory School in Navan, a superior school which has a scholarship available for any student with proper qualifications. This student will be selected from our National School with the recommendation of the headmaster. Your son, Mr. Ledwidge has received that recommendation."

Francis trembled—his face scarlet with embarrassment—and his heart raced with pride. Never before had anyone spoken with such approval of him. "Imagine—a poet!" He had read Burns and Wordsworth—but to be thought of as one of them – he, Francis Ledwidge, whose foolish verses for pleasure or in pain were considered poetry by the master! Patrick spoke at last. He chose his words sparingly. "I need my son to learn the farm—to be able to support himself by the land, sir. For you to fill his head with thoughts as you speak is foolish. Of what good is this education? You barely support yourself master. Fortunate for you, you live with your widowed mother."

The master's voice in agitation interrupted. "We are not discussing my situation, Mr. Ledwidge, I speak of the future for Francis. Whatever fortune has ordained his life means much more than being a ploughman all his life."

"Good evening to you, schoolmaster," said Patrick. "My boy is my business. I shall not promise he will attend any school. His lessons are to be learned here with me on the farm; the lessons a farmer must know to keep his roof in good order, his stables and livestock clean. He will keep his eyes on the earth and not the stars."

Francis leaned against the wall, its rough surface against his cheeks now wet with tears. Something inside him grew dim. The darkness of the kitchen matched the sudden darkness of his mind. Now he was totally alone. There was no one who knew him or cared to know him. The front door closed. Mr. Madden had gone.

The week passed, and Francis with heavy heart did the chores as directed with a listlessness that betrayed his broken spirit. Conversation between father and son was only regarding the quality of his labors and of the tasks he was assigned.

The spring was rainy. Cool winds kept the boy to the cottage. No books other than school texts, which the master had given him for self study were his companions. He had been permitted to school only six days since the conversation between the master and his father. He had given no sign that he had heard what passed between his father and Mr. Madden. He remembered that the master had been cordial enough to him on those days which he had attended classes, but the master's eyes were full of sadness. His manner, Francis thought, was a bit forced as if he were embarrassed being so deeply rejected by the conversation with Francis' father. Mr. Madden would think to himself when looking at the lad, "A common ploughman, gifted by God with that radiant soul, the father is killing the lad's spirit under manure and potato peelings. Good God, what justice is there in this world?"

On the last day of term, Francis' father permitted him to attend the final session. He was up before dawn to do his chores. The father watched his stoic figure with lantern in hand lighting a small patch against the blueblack sky, as he made his way to the stable. Completing his duties he returned to the kitchen where he wrapped a large slice of bread in his kerchief, gathered his school books under his arm, and started down the path towards the school house. The sun rose behind the Wicklow Mountains in the east. Droplets of dew lying on tufts of grass reflecting its silvered glory brought Francis to a halt. He put his book down on the pebbled roadway and walked towards the fragile illuminated knoll. Putting his hand out he touched the dawn that lingered on his fingertips for seconds only and then was gone. Within him something stirred. It was as if he were newly placed upon the earth where no pain nor fear nor anger ever dwelled. All his young being now knew that within himself beauty also dwelt. Within his soul he would always find it there and no one could take it from him.

## The National School

Promptly at nine o'clock the school master entered the classroom. Scraping stools came to attention. Through an open window, close by the road, came the piercing call of a blackbird. All heads turned as one—so startling was the sound. Francis alone kept his eyes on the master. The master too had not been looking out the window but at his young charge. Each smiled a greeting of welcome and farewell. Soon the class, the last, was over. The children in high spirits having concluded their academic endeavors for the term, now spilled happily into the school yard and eagerly looked forward to celebrating a summer free from the ties of the world of books.

Francis moved quietly from his place towards the master's desk which sat upon a square platform.

"Francis, I never told you about the scholarship you were to receive to the Priory School in Navan." Mr. Madden spoke wearily and with a great sadness.

"I heard sir, I was in the kitchen; I heard it all," Francis said with head bowed.

The master paled. "You heard all?"

"Yes, sir, it hurt me greatly but now I have found out something about myself I never knew."

"Will you share that something with me?" inquired the master hesitantly.

He smiled. "Sir, it is your faith and belief in me—in those words you spoke to my father."

The master looked earnestly at his pupil. "If I have done that my boy, my life behind this desk has meaning."

He reached into his pocket and withdrew a small parcel wrapped in brown paper and tied with cord. "This is for you, Francis—to read if you will during the summer." The boy shyly loosened the cords and slid the paper back. The cover was plain—nothing printed upon it. He turned to the first page where was written in the master's hand—Francis Ledwidge, his book. Francis looked up with joyous eyes and then glanced down to turn the pages—all empty—waiting for an author—He!

The summer passed languidly and Francis, when time allowed, would climb the valley to Ballynock. There in fair or rainy weather he would gaze out over the verdant pastures toward the mountains. His companions were the ever present notebook and the sometimes passing squirrel, or a distant horse resting in the shade from the noon heat. The village children were far away in the meadow below, skylarking. Francis was content unto himself.

## Aunt May Ann

One late summer afternoon when Francis had finished in the stable, he found his father at the front gate with his Aunt, Mary Ann. Aunt Mary Ann lived in Navan and once or twice a year would descend quite accidentally, being in the district visiting a friend as she would say, upon the Ledwidges.

Aunt Mary Ann was a plump woman with skin as pink and white as a young girl. She always wore black and made a rustling sound when she moved, propelled as she was by taffeta petticoats. She was in her late sixties but of mind and nature much younger. Her eyes lit when she saw Francis. Her heart sympathized with the lad, knowing of the cold and dark nature of Patrick and the warm and shy ways of his son.

"Francis, you've been on my mind for so long. I decided to come see you." She threw her arms about him and he disappeared into the rustle and warmth of her robust frame. Putting her bonnet back into place after the embrace and tucking a stray silver lock under her hat, she reached into the trap and lifted out a wicker hamper which she promptly put into Patrick's hesitant arms.

"Now let us go in and have some tea. There is a cake in the hamper and I can't wait for you to sample it." The little group moved indoors with Francis taking a backward look, to see if her pony was properly secured. The parlor was cool and full of the scent of heliotrope. The curtainless windows were picture frames for the wild roses growing over the stone fence. Soon the kettle was singing and emitting small puffs of smoke signalling all was ready for the feast. Francis seldom, except on occasions such as this, ever tasted cake. He was so pleased with such a treat that he was hopeful he might be encouraged to have more than one slice! Aunt Mary Ann having sipped her tea, was eager to hear of any news that might be forthcoming.

"Patrick," she began, "I heard from Mr. Madden's mother that your Francis was to be the scholar recommended to be sent to the Priory on a scholarship and that you refused."

At last Patrick realized why she had come—the busybody.

"That's my business Mary Ann!", he answered tersely.

"Well, I find it hard to believe a Ledwidge would turn his back on such a grand opportunity for the lad's future." Francis cleared his throat and asked to be excused. He made a mumbled mention about giving the pony hay and water before the long trip back. Mary Ann and Patrick didn't seem to hear. He shut the door quietly and went to the pump to get the water and escape whatever ensued.

Mary Ann drew herself up in a manner of a captain of a ship giving general orders to those under her command.

"Patrick Ledwidge, you've a stone for a heart, the lad will grow to hate you with you showing him no love but only the threat of the stick. He has no woman to soften the hurts that come. Surely man, you can see that."

Patrick leaned forward in his chair and spoke carefully. "Mary Ann, I know it's a sad and lonely existence for the boy, but I've got to harden him to his lot in life. He's a farmer's son and it's to the soil he must attend. When he's a man, it's not a book that will clean the chimney or tend the livestock or add a few acres to the farm. I don't want his head to be filled with words that no one will hear or care to read. That's my final word."

"Patrick Ledwidge, you'll live to regret it. Have you ever thought of sending him to America? Your late wife's sister, Nan, lives there and she would welcome her sister's boy. She was so fond of her sister. Remember?"

Patrick looked into his empty tea cup and ran his fingers around edge, thinking of old memories of the two colleens, Nan and Duveen—heaven rest her soul. Like twins they were—dark and lively and laughter surrounding them. His Duveen—he smiled remembering her—maybe it was the answer. It would give the boy a chance. Would he ever see the boy again? Perhaps this separation would save them both. He loved the lad but it was hard for him to show tenderness. "What think you, Patrick?"

He stood slowly and moved toward the front window. He looked out upon the son he found so hard to know. He studied the boy's blonde hair against the ruddy face making small talk to the pony. He watched his sturdy arm patting the pony's mane and saw him laughing at some little joke he had said to the animal. Patrick remembered now that Nan had children. Would she have Francis after so many years? Questions turned about in his head. What about the farm? Would the boy come back—no never—if he goes now I may never see him again. Patrick's head lifted and he spoke sharply.

"I'll put it to the lad."

"Better before you do that, to let me write to Nan and see if she'll have him. Have you the money to send him?"

"Yes, I have the money," Patrick sighed.

"Enough for his return?"

"That will be his own doing—then I'll know he really wants to come home," replied Patrick.

"You poor man!," Mary Ann rose and walked to his side. "Did you ever say I love you to anyone dear to your heart?"

He turned and walked quickly to the door. "Many times," he answered sadly, "long ago, but I don't know if she heard me."

"Above me in their hundred schools
the magpies bend their young to rules
and like an apron full of jewels
the dewy cobweb swings"

## The Letter

In those days, in country districts, the postman came once a week and many times letters for his district were few if any at all. His arrival at a village cottage was a special event worthy of all the family to stop work immediately and read what wondrous or sad news had come to them.

It was in late August that summer that the postman knocked on Ledwidge's door with the letter from America. Here was the answer to Mary Ann's inquiry about Francis' future. Ledwidge himself came to the door and received it. He had never mentioned the conversation between himself and Mary Ann to his son. First he should know if Nan would want the boy. The postman waited hoping to get some idea as to what news came over the ocean to that "hermit". Sure the fellow never got a letter from anyone in all the years I've been delivering, mused the postman, his eyes scrutinizing Patrick's face.

Patrick closed the door without thanking the postman who turned quickly uttering his sentiments in one word, "Boor!"

Francis had gone to the meadow to check the fence line and would not be back for sometime, so Patrick went to the kitchen and tore open the letter. Without sitting, he read the contents aloud.

Dear Patrick,

    It was a great surprise to hear from Mary Ann. Having heard nothing from her or you in many years I feared you were no longer on this earth! She told me of your Francis and of hers and your hope that the young lad might come to America to live with me and my family someday.

    You know that I have five children, four girls and one boy. My husband has an employment agency and we do quite well. I shall always keep my dear sister, Duveen, close to my heart. Hearing of her son's lonely life without mother, brothers, or sisters, I truly welcome him to come and be with us. Mary Ann tells me he is an intelligent lad and does well in his studies. Grand—Mary Ann also states you will pay his fare here. As to the future, that shall be in Francis' hands. Please let me know the particulars as to his arrival.

    Your loving sister-in-law,
    Nan O'Hanlon

Done with the stroke of a pen! Patrick felt a tightening sensation in his throat. "I've signed him to something I know nothing about—a life I have no way of foreseeing. No one of his own to turn to." With those words Patrick realized he too was speaking about himself.

    After the supper dishes had been put away and the fire banked for the night, Patrick called the boy into the parlor. Now this was unexpected and the parlor at that! Francis had a foreboding that something very important must have happened—and it had. Patrick brought the lamp from the kitchen and motioned the boy to seat himself. "Francis," Patrick came to the point. "We've not been close as father and son. I am sorry for that. It may be our natures that are at fault, if I may call it a fault. I know you were greatly disappointed when I forbade you to go to Navan on the scholarship, and even discouraged you from attending school regularly. You see, my boy, it has always been my plan for you to follow in the ways of the Ledwidge's—close to the soil. But I see it is not your way."

Francis remained silent. He was stunned. He had never heard his father go on in this way. Could it be he would never permit him to attend school next term? Patrick seeing the disillusionment in the boy's face proceeded.

"My boy, your Aunt Mary Ann and I have sent a letter to your mother's sister in America. Nan O'Hanlon is her name. We asked Nan if she might let you come and live with her and her family." Whatever Patrick said after that was not heard. The words "to America—to America" spun round and round in the boy's head. His heart raced. A myriad of thoughts came up and he answered them. All answers were "yes—yes." Patrick stopped and looked at the boy. Had he heard him? His cheeks were scarlet. His eyes reflected the excitement his body felt.

"Can I go, Da?"

Patrick's heart sank. "So eager—have I made him so unhappy that the lad fairly bolts from his chair to pack his few clothes and leave me," he thought. A passerby pauses and looks from the roadway into the lighted window. A scene of family life, warm and loving he beholds—a man and his young son engaged in conversation. The young boy with joyous smile and father looking at him with fatherly devotion warms the onlooker's heart as he passes on down the lane. Better you came when you did and went your way traveler, than to know the truth!

The days dawned clear and beautiful in those weeks following Patrick's news of America. Francis had not slept well these past weeks. His mind was a kaleidoscope of pictures of people and familiar places. He took trips to his fortress at Ballynock and gazed at the fields and mountains intently, hoping to store in his mind all of his native land—perhaps forever.

One evening as Francis knelt before the kitchen hearth to start a fresh fire for the cool September evening, his father looked up from his chair and said quietly.

"My son, there are many things I have not said to you which I find hard now to say. Good bye is not the right word because it is final and

I hope to have you back with me someday." He paused sighing, "If they, that is your aunt or her husband, treat you unkindly, write your Da."

It was the first time he had said that word. It lingered on his lips. Francis looked up into Patrick's tired eyes and said, "Da, don't worry. I shall write you every week and tell you all that happens to me." He paused, for he felt it hard to swallow. "I may even become the farmer you want me to be." Patrick looked down into the clear blue eyes and placed his hand gently on the shoulder which trembled visibly. "Only if it is your wish my son." The touch of that sturdy hand on his shoulder gave silent testimony of that poor heart's tenderness. It moved the boy visibly. He threw his arms around his father's waist and with his head against his father's heart whispered, "Da-Da."

## America

September twenty-sixth dawned rainy and windy. Francis, age ten years and four months, would leave Ireland on the British ship, Franconia, bound from the Port of Cobh to the City of New York on Saturday, the twenty-sixth day of September in the year 1898. His carpetbag contained one suit, a Confirmation gift from the master a few years before. His father had given him a green woolen cap. His Aunt Mary Ann had given him her husband's gold watch to be clipped to his inside vest by a thin network of chain. The trap which Patrick hired was late and when the two had put the tarpaulin over their heads to shelter them from the driving rain, they had to urge the driver to use all speed to get them to Cobh harbor in time for the tender which would take the young passenger to the ship.

The trap lurched along the pebbled roadway with dispatch. As it rounded the corner to the village, the highway turned to cobblestone, and the trap swayed precariously threatening to dump its soggy passengers into a ditch. As it came abreast of the National School, the driver slowed to a trot and then pulled up to a halt. There, in the gateway, with a black umbrella sheltering him from the deluge, stood Mr. Madden.

Francis felt a sense of guilt for he hadn't said good-bye to him. It was too painful. His heart beat fast as the master hurried to the trap and extended his hand to him.

"Godspeed Francis. Don't forget your old master." Then he backed off and turned toward the school. Inside the tarpaulin, Francis' tears spilled over the gold five dollar piece left in his hand. Patrick turned his head aside and with a snap of the whip the driver urged the trap onward.

The passengers reached Cobh with but twenty minutes to spare. The rain hurtled by the wind, struck the passengers with such force that father and son held fast to one another to get their breath. The driver, muffled in his Macintosh, jumped off the vehicle, and bending low into the wind led his pony to the shelter of an inn near the dock but a few feet away.

There bobbing in the quay was the tender. The ship was painted green with white trim and seemed determined to withstand all that the Atlantic Ocean might do to dash it to the bottom of the harbor like a toy. As Patrick and his son slowly made their way to the gangplank, a voice called out from above the waves and general furor.

"Hurry lads, it's up anchor a soon as you come aboard." Francis and Patrick looked up, eyes crouched against the weather, at the most incongruous sight one could ever expect to see under these dire circumstances! The head, extending from a circular pedestal in the center of the tender, was wearing a black derby! How it stayed on its rotund master one could only wonder. For the first time in many months both Ledwidges laughed heartily and the storm within and without seemed less fearful.

Once aboard the tender all was made ready to get underway. In the shelter of the stern were a few passengers huddled together on a long slatelike bench steadying themselves against the onslaught of the waves. Above the din of the storm would come shouts of the captain who was exposed to the elements literally from the waist up, shouting orders to his yellow- slickered hands. The sight of him would remain with the boy for the rest of his life. The jolly round face, the black derby standing singularly alone in the fury of the storm was undefeated and glorious!

In a short time, the wind lessened and the rocking of the tender became less violent. The captain had less to say to the crew, and the passengers sensed the worst was over. The time was close to four and the tender was scheduled to meet the Franconia at four-thirty. The sky led one to believe they might have missed her in the fog, but the captain assured them that she would be visible. The fellow was a man of his word, and suddenly the bow and the lighted portholes peered through the grey fog. Within minutes the grandeur of this mighty ship of the line rose complete before them.

The gangplank was creakingly lowered and attached to the tender deck by the "black derby's" deckhands. The time of parting had come. The four passengers with luggage and hat boxes, all seasoned voyagers, moved quickly up the gangplank to the ship. Patrick was struck dumb. He had gone over in his mind what to say. All of what had proceeded was so strange and unreal that the practiced farewell was forgotten. Francis, aware of the reality now of the parting, was also full of sadness. He was nearly overcome with despair. Then from high above on the Franconia deck, a seaman shouted, "Hurry up down there. We'll be under way in a minute." Francis grasped his carpetbag from his father's hand and then dropped it. He threw his arms around Patrick and both father and son, in that one clumsy embrace, said good-bye.

Francis grasped the railing and moved up the gangplank without turning. He could barely see the planking and the ocean moving beneath his feet. At last he reached the deck and the sailor who had previously shouted his minute warning lifted the boy on to the deck. The gangplank was lifted, moved through an opening, and then disappeared. A huge steel door closed the gaping hole and sealed it for the journey. The anchor cable turned and slowly lifted. The little tender bobbed in the swell. Patrick moved to the uncovered lower deck of the tender searching above for one last glimpse of his son. Looking desperately he now turned his head towards the stern of the ship, and there on the open deck, stood a lone figure waving. He saw the green cap!

The little tender receded into a fog bank all too swiftly and was gone. Francis' land of birth was no longer visible to him. A few seagulls screeched their farewell, then swooped high and made their way toward the shore. The green-capped figure wished he could encircle their necks and by some miracle ride the wind back home with them.

Francis Ledwidge left his native land with one small carpetbag, his steerage ticket, and a green woolen cap. He ate his meals in a crowded, overheated cabin in the bottom of the ship. The people around him had families and were eagerly talking about their life in the new land, America. A heaviness of spirit lay upon the boy. He felt a desolation to the marrow of his bones. It was hard to believe that in this mass of humanity not one gentle hand lay upon his—no eyes of kindness or a caring look assured him that there was hope and destiny in his future.

As the days passed his mind turned toward the welcome to await him. Who were these unknown people into whose care his father had given him?

On the eighth day of October the Franconia steamed into New York harbor. The steerage passengers were permitted to gather their meager baggage and to proceed for their exodus from the third class deck. Francis inched closer to the ship's railing to get his first glimpse of this new world. The day was glorious. The cobalt sky with mountainous cumulus clouds drifted over the distant city. There in the harbor entrance a magnificent statue stood as a sentinel. Who was she? "That's the statue of Liberty," someone replied. As the ship drew closer Francis' breath came in short gasps. He had never seen such a statue before. "It's the Blessed Mother," he whispered to himself, "it's something like the one in St. Brendan's but oh so much larger." He was almost directly in front of her now and his eyes filled with tears as the ship passed slowly up the harbor to its berth. "Mother of God protect me," he murmured. The liner's whistle blasted her welcome to the little tugs who had placed themselves on each side of her. The tugs echoed the greeting with their own sharp brisk salute. Francis knew he was not quite as alone as he had thought. Looking back toward the lady, he always remembered that it was she who had been first to welcome him to America!

Although the steerage passengers were the last to disembark, the mood of everyone was cheerful and full of expectation. Francis checked to see that he still had his name card that Aunt Mary Ann had given him on his lapel. He swung down the gangplank to the dock stopping several times to see if any person below was wearing a white carnation, the badge for identification for Nan!

Shouts of greetings came from all directions. His head turned from side to side. Some were pushing forward to grasp loved ones; some gave sobs of joy for long unseen friends. The crowd moved slowly towards the custom lines. Efficient black-garbed men with matching black-visored caps with a red C circled on breast pockets opened the luggage. They took but a minute for Francis. The agent tapped him gently and said, "Move on lad."

Francis walked away from the surging mass and put his carpetbag down. The people from Ireland passed through the gates and spilled on to the street slowly moving away from the dock on their way to a new and unknown world.

Had there been some mistake in the correspondence—the wrong date or the liner perhaps! Impossible!

Soon the custom agents folded away their long tables and hurried off into the afternoon. Francis sat down on his carpetbag and waited.

"Francis, Francis," a voice split the silence and echoed the length of the pier. The sound of heels tapping quickly followed and there, running towards him, was a lady wearing the white carnation. He stood up pulling his cap off respectfully as the figure came closer. She was smiling and extending her hand to him. "I'm Nan of course," she smiled. He liked her immediately!

While on the train ride home to Connecticut Nan explained her tardiness. "New York traffic is impossible," she laughed shaking her head. "I could have walked there faster." She squeezed his hand and continued her non-stop monologue. She had a gaiety which gave her a special radiance. She liked him too. He could sense that. "I don't know where to begin Francis about the arrangements, you know. I'm sure you'll get along with your cousins. I have a son, Joe, two years older than you. He's glad you've come since he's outnumbered with four sisters!"

"A family at last!" thought Francis! The train lurched side to side and the little wood stove shifted dangerously with it but managed each time to do its duty to heat the chilly car and remain upright.

In the hour and a half that Nan had been with him, Francis sensed a wellness of being that he had never felt before. The conductor walked through the car and announced, "Stamford next stop," Francis could hardly contain the newly discovered happiness that flooded his being. The train slowed, grunted and finally ground to a stop before a small but neat little station. He lifted his carpetbag from the rack standing on tip toe to reach it, he brushed off the green velvet seat leaving no footprints behind.

Nan grasped his hand and they moved towards the steps. There on the platform facing him were five young faces. He stumbled down the steps and put out his hand.

"I'm Francis Ledwidge," his voice broke a bit. They smiled broadly back at him. He turned to Nan. She put her arm over his shoulder and drew him close and said, "Welcome home, Francis!"

## Home

Stamford, Connecticut, was a small, but growing industrial town bounded on the east by Long Island Sound. The cobbled streets spread out like the spokes of a wheel, the center of which encompassed the Town Hall, the Presbyterian Church, several stores and a foundry, down near the harbor. Francis's eyes, accustomed to broad fields and high mountains and the distances of a mile or more between neighboring cottages, thought this Stamford appeared a metropolis!

Next he saw his first miracle—a car! Mr. Rutledge, of Rutledge and Marshall, the town's most important Foundry, could be seen driving his black Stanley to the Presbyterian Church with his family each Sunday. Francis knew instinctively he must be in a very wealthy community!

Greyrock Place, Francis' new home, was a three-storied duplex with large rooms throughout. Inside it had a magnificent mahogany staircase which led to the second floor. The carving of each pedestal in the staircase seemed like the work of a gifted artisan. The first floor was rented to two gloomy school teachers. Francis' new home was the second floor. As he climbed the stairs he fingered the staircase railing with awe. The beautiful, uncarpeted stairs were waxed to a high gloss, and a rainbow stained-glass window on the landing caught the setting sun and lit up the hallway with the glory of that of a cathedral.

In those first days, Francis slept in a double bed with his cousin Joe. As time and circumstance developed in the following months, he found himself moved to the third floor in a storage area with a small cot and washstand which his cousin Joe referred to as the attic!

How this happened was difficult to ascertain. Perhaps it began with the warmth which Nan showered on the little orphan as his cousins called him. They ignored the fact that he had a father!

Nan's husband, Joseph O'Hanlon, was a stoic man. He was seemingly detached from his family and eager to get to his black horsehair chair in the evening, cross his skinny legs, and envelop himself in reading the newspaper. Francis would remember Mr. O'Hanlon as always dressed in dark grey or dark brown suits with high spotlessly white plastic collars and dark cravats. His black hair parted in the middle, and his grey complexion gave him a funereal appearance. His children tended to ignore him.

But Nan—what loveliness and liveliness she possessed! Francis marveled at her. She seemed always smiling, pushing her light brown hair back against her head and always ready to break into a song or a dance step whenever the mood prevailed. He had never known another like her. Her children seemed embarrassed by her for some reason. Perhaps because they were conniving, self-centered creatures intent on promoting self. Any sign of gaiety was looked upon as frivolous.

Francis tried to make friends with his cousins, but each of them seemed to look down their thin pinched noses at him in ridicule. He had written his father of his impressions of his surroundings but only of the wonders of his new world , not the sadness that it had for him.

His school days occupied most of his days, but his attic room was a restful refuge from the activity on the second floor where his loud, distasteful cousins romped and cavorted.

One morning in early spring, seven months after his arrival, he awoke to a light tapping upon the attic door. It was still dark as he looked out the small paned window. He wrapped the comforter around himself and went to the door. Standing there under the single bulb which was illuminating the landing, stood Nan, dressed in slippers and bathrobe.

"May I come in Francis. I want to talk to you before anyone is about." He stood and watched her as she walked to the window.

"Come here Francis and sit down," she spoke softly. From her robe pocket she took an envelope and pulled out a letter.

"It's from your father." The very first letter from Da—and he sent it to Nan. Francis felt a bitterness well up within him. She unfolded the letter and in a whispered voice read:

Dear Sister-in-Law,

    I'm writing this letter to you in the hope you will give its message to my son. I have met and married a decent woman named Sarah O'Fairlain five months ago. She lived in Navan and I met her in the village where she was visiting. She has three young boys aged two, six, and ten. It has been a lonely life for me with Francis gone and no one of my own. Sarah feels that it is best the boy remain with you and family and make his way in America. I will send his dowry of ten pounds which is all I can afford. He is a strong lad and will earn his keep in the future I'm sure. I wish him well. I thank you for having him.

   Respectfully,

   Patrick Legwidge

Abandoned. Sold for ten pounds. Never to see Ballynock again and forgotten by his father, who at the whim of a new wife, would not himself write to his own son but tell a stranger to tell him he was unwanted.

The room glowed now with the morning sun but the figure seated so dejectedly never moved. Nan, her hands trembling, put the letter into her pocket. Better he not read those words again and again, trying to find somewhere written the sadness Patrick had not expressed. A father giving his son away with no hope of return—a ten-year-old child! She turned and sat next to the boy. Reaching her hand over his she said, "Francis lad, I'm sure your father meant well. This is a great country with much opportunity for such a fine lad as yourself."

Silence.

"A few more years and you can start work in Mr. O'Hanlon's office just like your cousins. You'll be part of O'Hanlon's Insurance and Employment Agency some day!," her voice faded.

Francis, with closed eyes sat with the comforter around his slumped shoulders.

"If only I had known my mother. I'm sure she wouldn't have done this to me," he whispered.

Nan stood, touched his bent head gently and left the room weeping—closing the door softly behind her.

## The Clock

Time and seasons passed as the ticking of a clock. Francis grew tall and slender—his body hardened by chopping and splitting logs for the fireplaces in winter. His muscles strengthened by lifting and moving furniture from room to room each time Nan redecorated. A handyman had replaced the little orphan. His cousins moved into social spheres into which he was not invited. His clothes were those passed down from Joe. His presence at meals was the second shift now. He ate with Hannah the cook and Martin, the newly acquired chauffeur for the new car Mr. O'Hanlon had purchased. He made no complaint. He lived in the attic room remote from sharp tongues and sly glances.

During these youthful years, Francis Ledwidge had dreamed of going home. He had written Aunt Mary Ann and that noble lady had been his only correspondent. His schoolmaster, Mr. Madden had died of the consumption. Only his widowed mother and a few students had stood by his grave at St. Brendan's to bid him farewell. Aunt Mary Ann would seldom mention his father in her letters except once two years before to say now he had twin step sisters. Mary Ann never visited Ledwidge.

Nan's liveliness and gaiety seemed to decline as the years passed. Her laughter was infrequent and her only pleasure was to sit in good weather in the garden Francis had planted for her beside the garage and to talk with him there. He spoke to her about the books he was reading and shared with her his childhood recollections of the National School, his mountain fortress at Ballynock, and the loss and longing for it all.

"Francis lad, I want you to know something," she said one spring morning in the garden. "I'm not well. I don't believe I shall ever know good health again. I want you to know how much you mean to me. There is, I believe, between some people a chemistry that brings their spirits closer together than others. It is this way between us. It need not be explored only recognized. I know you care little for the business. You know your cousins and their ambitions. I tell you, Francis, I wish to God you were mine. The pride I feel for you far surpasses that for my own children. God help me for saying it. They are a scheming lot—the whole pack of them. But I've set aside something for you dear boy. It is in my will."

The afternoon sun dipped below the horizon and a coolness settled over the garden. Nan rose. "Eat with me tonight in my sitting room, Francis. We'll talk more." He stood as she walked slowly inside—a fading lovely woman—the only one in the world outside of Mary Ann who cared truly about him.

## The Will

Francis awoke to loud voices a few months later. It must have been the middle of the night but no, it was only eleven thirty. He had gone to bed early. He opened his door and went down the stairs to the entrance of the kitchen door. He looked in. No one was there. They were all in the dining room at the table. He couldn't help but hear.

"Mother, it's insanity. He's not our brother. Your mental state should be considered. This is downright irrational." Joe's voice was high and nearly hysterical.

"Mother, Francis is not immediate family," Margaret, the oldest daughter interjected. "He is a first cousin, a handyman, a thick, stupid serf who embarrasses us with his farmer's presence." Nan, her voice high and trembling said, "Enough – enough! It is my wish and I shall have my way most definitely."

Francis turned and closed the kitchen door quietly behind him and went down the back hall leading to the street. His eyes filled with tears and his cheeks were burning. Oh for Ballynock on this night.

In the few years that Francis had lived in America he had made no true friends. As leisure time was rare, he usually could be found reading at the library or filling a paper bag with more books to take home.

Mr. O'Hanlon spent all of his time in the office now. Joe, his heir, knowing the dynasty would fall inevitably into his open and receptive hands, spent summers close on his father's heels learning the business. The girls with the exception of Ann who resembled Nan physically and spiritually, were waiting in the wings to share their birthright with their revered brother.

He knew something was very wrong the moment he turned onto Greyrock Place upon his return later one morning in the late summer.

Mr. O'Hanlon's black car was parked in front of the house and it was only ten o'clock in the morning. Mr. O'Hanlon didn't usually arrive until dinner time at six o'clock. Francis hurried up the back steps and entered the kitchen door. Hannah, the cook sat in the corner with her large white apron covering her face. At the sound of the door closing she looked up. He knew at that moment that the one and only friend he had was gone. Hannah threw herself into Francis' arms sobbing bitterly. "Only the good die young, master Francis." He gently led her back to the chair and placed her tenderly down into it.

"She was here, right here, where you is standing, master Francis, talking with me about the lamb roast for dinner. I seen her sway a little then she fell into my arms." Hannah moaned, "I dragged her to her room as best I could. She was light as a feather. I kept calling her name. She never spoke a word. I got her on the bed and ran to the telephone to call for help. But I knew I was too late." Here Hannah lifted her apron to her face and continued sobbing.

Francis went through the dining room into the parlor where his cousins and Mr. O'Hanlon sat, solemn-faced and speechless. They never looked at him.

"I'm truly sorry," he stammered searching for words. They never responded. As he turned to go to his room, Ann rose and followed him to the door. She whispered, "She loved you, Francis," and touched his arm gently. He turned and with tears falling unashamedly he asked, "May I see her for a moment, Ann?" She nodded. He followed the slight form so reminiscent of her mother to the bedroom. On the bed, with a comforter covering all but the beloved face, was the only person who had shown this hapless boy kindness. He walked to the bed and stood looking at her. "Good-bye Nan. I'll always think of you as my mother." The last word lingered longer than the others. He remembered her as he first had seen her, heard her heels tapping, her voice calling—"Francis—I'm Nan of course." He reached out and touched her hair, bent and kissed her forehead and whispered so only she could hear—"Good-bye Mother."

Nan O'Hanlon left to Francis Ledwidge, her beloved nephew, the sum of five thousand dollars. When Gregory MacMahon, the family lawyer, read that clause in the will in the O'Hanlon parlor, Nan had reached down and with a final gesture gave to Francis the greatest gift of all—his freedom. There was nothing the family could do but accept it. Mr. O'Hanlon had known all along. It was to him a small price for which to be rid of a future irritant. He never crossed Nan when she had put it into her will. He felt the young man would no longer be underfoot. He never meant for him to be the handyman and he knew local tongues had long poked fun at his treatment of a family relative. Francis, his cheeks burning hearing of the words Nan had written "her beloved nephew" and of the amount which was far beyond what he could ever conceive, turned his head to the window in the parlor and put his hand to his mouth to stifle the sob which escaped in spite of all.

Seven years and two months from that ominous day that he had left his home for the new world, he sailed back to Ireland. He never heard further word about his father and new family, nor had he made any effort to correspond with the father who had in Francis' mind abandoned him. He felt no regret leaving the little town that he had first looked upon with such hope nor any sentiment of his cousins, except of course for Ann. Francis had written to Aunt Mary Ann and she had written him welcoming him to her home for as long as he might want to stay. Seventeen years he had lived on this earth and had only two who cared if he lived or died. One was now gone and the other—the durable old auntie who welcomed him into her home.

Mr. O'Hanlon was at the dock to bid him farewell. They had driven from Stamford in style with Martin at the wheel. Francis, the ill clad young man and the dapper Mr. O'Hanlon who had cultivated a black mustache and neat, short beard, which he felt gave him more distinction, made a study in contrasts.

As Francis stood on the boat deck, with his familiar carpetbag still servicing his small needs, he looked down into the faces of the crowd below him. He saw arms raised in farewell, paper ribbon ricochetting up and down from deck to dock. He thought if only one face down there could truly care for him—for Francis Ledwidge! Mr. O'Hanlon had not waited for the departure of the ship as he had an appointment in Stamford.

The ship moved effortlessly into the harbor. The people left the railing to inspect their accommodations. Soon only Francis was left to watch the receding skyline etched against the horizon. There she was. The Statue of Liberty. He looked upon her expressionless face and thought how wise the sculptor was to have made her so. Each could read into the face his own emotions as he passed by her. This time he smiled and turned his eyes toward the open sea. In his heart he felt at last he was going home. His remembrance of Liberty as The Blessed Mother upon his arrival had been forgotten!

He had decided to go directly to Southhampton to disembark. He wondered after all the years which had passed if that indefatigable tender master with the black derby still reigned triumphant in his little lookout station on the green and white tug in Cobh!

On the last evening on board ship, Francis took an after dinner stroll. He had traveled frugally in tourist class. He thought that after having first crossed the Atlantic in steerage, tourist class was the height of luxury. He enjoyed the clear September wind with its brisk snapping breeze off the Atlantic. Stars seemed somewhat closer to one aboard ship. His mind turned over the many ideas he had concerning plans once he was in Navan. First, he didn't want to be a burden to Mary Ann and yet he would welcome her kindness to him. He was seventeen years old. He had four thousand and five hundred dollars left from his inheritance. The future welcomed him, but his plans still held many uncertainties.

## Dunsany

As fortune has it, fate seems destined to move in ways the human mind can scarcely fashion or design—a corner not turned, an unrelated incident can change the course of our lives.

As Francis started down the stairway to the tourist deck, a man coming up stopped short of knocking both of them down, or up depending on the direction each was traveling.

"By jove." said the stranger. "Strange way to meet, no way can we avoid each other." Turning about, and bowing, the tall, dark-haired gentleman proceeded to the lower deck. Francis smiled to himself. Friendly fellow, he thought. Someone else might have barked a curse at the annoyance.

The stranger then put out his hand in introduction, "My name's Edward Drax Dunsany, young gentleman."

Francis smiled broadly at the distinguished looking man with bright, penetrating blue eyes.

"Francis Ledwidge, sir."

The evening passed quickly as these two strangers shared confidences as old friends might, leaning over the ship's rail gazing into the night. Francis unburdened his heavy soul upon the cushioning receptivity of a man who, but for a chance meeting, he might never have met.

It was just like Nan had said. There are some who have a chemistry...It was through this chemistry that Edward Dunsany, known in British peerage, as Lord Dunsany, entered the life of a young farm lad from County Meath. To no one had Francis felt so kindred as swiftly and surely as this, except Nan. Francis was unaware of Dunsany's title at this time but referred to him respectfully as sir or Mr. Dunsany. They made arrangements to meet for breakfast. The next morning Francis packed his few things and carried his carpetbag to the salon and joined Dunsany at his table.

Edward Dunsany was a descendent of the knights who had served in the Saxon Normandy War. The standard which flew from the staff of the turret of his ancestral home, Adare Manor in Limerick, was the same which was carried by the British Army at Cornwall.

His service to his government had been a devoted one. His greatest sorrow was the plight of the Irish. He wished to right the situation in some way but he had little voice in the Parliament.

He admired Parnell. He was torn between his love of country, England, and of the valiant Irish who had for centuries been deprived of their God-given right to independence.

There was something about this tall slender Irishman that caught Dunsany's imagination. His use of language as he described his life kept Dunsany rapt in attention. The pain and the joy in the youth's eyes were most moving. A natural orator, Dunsany mused. This Francis Ledwidge had the ability to move the heart and enrapture the mind with his thoughts in words that flowed so easily!

As the ship was to dock at noon, Francis and Dunsany moved through the salon toward the gangplank. They seated themselves in two deck chairs and continued their conversation.

"You see sir, I'm at a crossroads. There are several paths ahead for me and I must stop and consider which one to travel. First, I'd like to finish my education. I have a home for a time in Navan with my great aunt Mary Ann. Once there I shall make inquiries concerning a university."

Dunsany leaning forward asked, "Francis, have you ever considered running for public office?" Francis looked stricken.

"Public office Mr. Dunsany? Myself? Sir, what are my credentials! I'm a farm lad long gone from my district with no experience whatsoever in politics—no connections at all."

Dunsany smiled. "You have something that very few politicians possess lad. You have truth; you have a God given gift with words—you have a presence, if I may use that word, that captures an audience even if it be only one," he added with a smile.

Francis looked shocked. "Sir, you are most charitable but..."

Dunsany pounded his fist on the arm of the chair. "Nonsense Ledwidge. I speak the truth even if what I have said has been heard by myself alone!" The gong sounded for the passengers to disembark. Dunsany, realizing that Francis was startled and confused, reassured him by giving him his card. He then took a small leather folding case from his inside jacket pocket, slipped a small pen from the holder on the pad, and inquired as to where he might write his new friend. Francis gave him Mary Ann's address in Navan. The two men walked to the front of the dock. Dunsany had a car waiting for his arrival. A chauffeur opened the back door as Dunsany turned to Francis. "You'll be hearing from me soon Frances Ledwidge. I shall be anxious to hear your plans." Francis shook the extended hand enthusiastically." Thank you sir for listening to me. I hope I haven't imposed on your kind nature."

Dunsany looked steadily into the boy's eyes and brusquely said, "I won't forget you lad." The door closed and a hand lifted in parting, Dunsany was gone.

Francis stood rooted to the spot watching the car maneuver into the traffic. Then he muttered, "And I won't be forgetting you, sir."

The boat train to Dublin arrived on time. Francis stepped onto his native land and felt love and pride for the small island which rose within him and infused his spirit with well being. "An orator, a politician you are, Francis Ledwidge." He laughed aloud and then turned to see if anyone had overheard him. His fellow passengers however were unaware and unconcerned—and what if they had overheard the mutterings of a farm lad, it would be of little interest to them!

The street scene which greeted him was overwhelming! Never had he seen so many carriages and beautiful horses! There were several cars, their engines wheezing and bucking, moving cautiously in and out of the Dublin street, horns tooting warnings to pedestrians crossing back and forth. Francis was hoping to see O'Connell Street and looked about 'for signposts. The jostling crowd moved like a tide buffeting him, he finally spied a Bobby with his white-domed hat and polished boots. "Excuse me sir, I'm looking for O'Connell Square."

"That'll be three streets down lad," responded the officer cheerfully. But Francis, not wanting to miss the train home, dismissed his much desired excursion for another time.

The train ride to Navan gave him a chance to look a the countryside he loved so well. Small white cottages laced the green rolling hills. He saw the farmers racking hay in the meadows. It reminded him of a scene from an artist's canvas. The stone fences wound over and around the fields. The little train stations in the different villages were painted white with lovely names such as Genda Lagh and Wicklow—printed neatly on their wooden signs. He enjoyed the station masters each holding a watch which they looked at intently, but not really with conviction. Many times when the train stopped to let off passengers they would be talking to someone on the platform about the price of peat or the new village priest paying no attention to the time! There was in this land of his a place that allowed each man that opportunity of extending a pleasant exchange without the pressure of a schedule to be followed. A few minutes here and there made little difference to country time tables on this railroad!

"Navan, Navan," called out the conductor. At last Francis rose and picked up his belongings, opened the door of the coach compartment and stepped out onto the platform.

"Francis!" Mary Ann called out to him, voluminous and emitting taffeta rustlings, she threw herself toward her grandnephew who in turn braced himself for the warm and welcome embrace.

Her cheeks ruddy and her eyes awash in joyful tears, she held her nephew tightly then abruptly released him to scrutinize what the seven years had written on that dear face.

"You've got your mother's eyes, your father's youthful coloring, and from the sight of you, must inherit your grandfather's stature. It's tall you are lad!"

Francis smiled, "You've not changed one bit Mary Ann. You've grown younger with the years."

"And," Mary Ann winked, "You've inherited your great grandfather's silver tongue."

Francis loved her neat little house in Navan. He had his own room that looked over a tiny garden. The house was on a plot of land close to the village proper. Many an evening he and Mary Ann would sit before the fire in the parlor and he would tell her tales about America. He was not vindictive concerning his cousins, and passed lightly over all the painful remembrances. He built a shrine to the memory of Nan with his words of love for her.

Mary Ann had him repeat and repeat his meeting with Mr. Edward Dunsany, a fine and proper gentleman. He omitted Dunsany's suggestion or mention of his being a politician. He knew Mary Ann would no doubt there and then start plotting his political future.

He had his inheritance safely in the Navan bank. He paid Mary Ann, who though strongly opposing it, a sum for his lodging. She somehow always managed to return the sum with a new sweater or a stout pair of brogans. He in turn would find something to surprise her—a fragrant sachet he had seen in a shop window or the lovely sea conch which she placed on the parlor table next to which her cup of tea was always ceremoniously placed. It delighted her between sips to lift the conch and hear the distant sea right in her very own parlor!

## The Letter

One afternoon in early December, when the sky threatened the first snow, Mary Ann went to answer the knock on the door. There on the steps was Mr. O'Neil, the postman.

"Ah, Mr. O'Neil, won't you be coming in for a cup of tea. It's that bitter it is."

Mr. O'Neil held the envelope in one hand and was rubbing his arm and hopping from one foot to the other to warm himself.

"Thank ye, Mrs. Timmons, sure and I have no heat in me at all at all but l have one more stop and then it's home to the fire and a wee bit of jorum for this one." Handing Mary Ann the letter, he turned and walked quickly down the lane. Mary Ann stood looking at the envelope trying to imagine who on earth was sending her a letter now that Francis was home.

A blast of frigid air interrupted her reverie and sent her into the parlor closing the door to the polar elements. Taking her spectacles from the mantel she read the envelope:

Francis Ledwidge

Timmons Cottage

Navan

County Meath, Ireland

The stamp was British and the postmark Donegal. "It's from himself," Mary Ann whispered in awe. The gentleman hasn't forgotten the lad after all.

Many weeks had passed since Francis had last seen Edward Dunsany. He had been turning over in his mind what the future held for him. The life of the university was to be considered. He had the money now for it. He could use the coming summer to apply to Trinity College in Dublin. All that he had read in the Navan library had seemed to fit all his desire for the life of that great city and the queen of Ireland's universities. Yet, he hesitated not wanting to choose a course without a wiser and more experienced head than his own to make such a profound decision.

As he turned into the gate at Mary Ann's, that evening he never expected to find a letter from his shipboard companion. He had weeks ago dismissed the meeting as intriguing but on closer scrutiny a bit too dramatic, and on the nature of a lark on the part of the distinguished and mysterious Dunsany.

Mary Ann seated in her favorite chair sat facing the door her hands crossed over her heaving bosom clasping the letter. Francis hung his coat on the peg in the entry and turned with a smile at the expansible black and white collared cheshire cat purring with excitement before him.

"Francis it's come me boy! The letter from your fine gentleman postmarked from Donegal. The stamp is of the King himself in the corner." Himself being referred to with such disdain revealed her sentiments towards the bewiskered monarch, George the V.

Francis was caught by surprise, He had dismissed his meeting with Dunsany. Now with the letter in Mary Ann's hands, it made him question his judgement about people. Having spent too much time examining his conscience on the matter, he reached out eagerly to read the letter. Mary Ann was breathless with excitement. She leaned forward in her chair. He decided to include her in the reading. The stationery was folded in three sections to fit the envelope. As he unfolded the letter, he noticed a crest on the top sheet. Thinking his friend may have written it from his club or office he turned to the contents.

Francis, my new friend,

I have thought of our meeting often, but family and other personal obligations have been consuming much of my time these past weeks. The remembrance of our meeting and conversation however has never left my mind for long. I hope you will be able to spend a weekend at my home on the fifteenth of January.

I shall have my chauffeur, Charles, meet you at Donegal Station. He shall deliver you to Adare Manor. We shall have the opportunity to continue our conversation where we left off. I have much to tell you.

With all best wishes to yourself and your dear Aunt Mary Ann (I feel I know the lady already thanks to you).

Sincerely,

(Lord) Edward Drax Dunsany

Mary Ann gasped, "A Lord is it?" Francis was silent. Why had he never told him? Reason spoke as if in answer. Why should he? He had given his name. Perhaps he thought the title would intimidate the young man's conversation—perhaps overwhelm him.

"Inviting my nephew to his manor now and for a weekend and met in Donegal by his chauffeur no less."

"He said he wanted to be remembered to you dear aunt," he reminded her.

"Now what do you think of that? A Ledwidge, a farm lad talking to and invited by a Royal to his manor. What was the name of the manor, Francis?"

He looked at the letter now folded on the table. "Adare Manor," he said, his voice barely audible.

"Glory be to the saints, if your father hears that he'll come to his senses and see what royalty thinks about his son."

Francis' excitement and his thoughts concerning the visit came to a halt at this remark. Never once, since he had returned, had he thought of visiting his father. Few miles separated them, but the pain of that letter of long ago dulled Ledwidge's desire to revisit his father now. Outside the window, large snow flakes fluttered in the wind and the turf fire grew noisy. He rose and adjusted the flue.

Mary Ann, her mind full of plans for the journey of one of her own family to the manor house of a Lord, felt no desire to start the supper nor even to pour the tea. Her fantasy called for the appearance of an obedient servant who would enter by the pull of an imaginary bell cord, curtsy, and place the silver tea tray before the illustrious aunt and her nephew. She could see herself pouring tea into a china teacup.

"I'm not going."

Mary Ann gasped. "Not going, what's this?"

"There is no point to extend a kindness he no doubt feels obligated to perform. You can see for yourself he postponed writing all these weeks. I count it close to two months."

"But the dear man explained," Mary Ann all but stamped her foot. "If he didn't want to continue the friendship he would have written he was going away and didn't know when he'd return. Enough of this lad, you told me you felt a kinship between you and Lord Dunsany—like that kinship you felt between yourself and Nan!"

He walked to the window. The night outside had turned white! The Lamplights cast golden silhouettes through the panes onto the chaste snow. He stood thinking of how suddenly and completely the world outside had changed since first he entered the door less than an hour before and how it might change again if he did visit Lord Dunsany!

The following day was Sunday. Francis awoke early as was his habit, and rose to draw back the bedroom curtains. He looked out upon a scene that would have pleased even the most hardened of hearts. The snow lay thick and deep over the roadway, a sleigh with two grey horses was passing, making the only tracks to be seen.

The trees, their boughs bent low with the weight of the snow made lovely arches and the sun, rising as if by surprise, smiled radiantly on the thin crest of ice atop the drifts, setting off illuminations which dazzled the eye.

Francis, inhaling the aroma of Mary Ann's Sunday morning breakfast of sausage and biscuits, hurried in his dressing to arrive at the kitchen before such a masterpiece became cold.

Aunt Mary Ann with a woolen shawl wrapped around her shoulders sat eyeing her nephew with a solemn gaze. "Francis I've been thinking about your suit. I mean the one you'd be wearing to his Lordship's. I've seen a beautiful Herringbone tweed at the Drapers. It would make up into a grand outfit for you."

Francis gulping the hot tea nearly choked. "Now Auntie, the suit I bought before I returned is only a few months old. It's perfectly suitable for the occasion."

Mary Ann rose from the table drawing her shawl around herself in majestic dignity looking aghast at her nephew's reply. "You'll not be going with one suit. You'll bring disgrace on the name of Ledwidge and Timmons. Then there'll be changes to be made between one meal and another—breakfast and dinner I hear."

"Auntie, Edward invited me, not my wardrobe. He knows me to be a farmer and with good fortune one who may have future expectations still unknown. Now don't let us pursue this any further."

Mary Ann, lifting the dishes from the table stood looking out the tiny paned window upon the lovely scene outside in silence.

"I'm thinking lad, you best get the horse and trap this morning, no walking to Mass on foot today."

Francis, his mind intent on the approaching week and the beauty outside had forgotten Mass! At this moment, he realized he had never thanked He who ordains the paths we walk, and is unnoticed until leisure permits us to look back and ask how it all had come to be.

He thought quickly of Nan, America, his inheritance, the return across the sea, Lord Edward Dunsany, and the staunch, loving figure so concerned from the beginning about his poor life, his Aunt Mary Ann.

He walked over to the one who always kept her eye upon the course he might take for the future. "You know upon deliberation you are quite right. A gentleman should have a change of clothes for the dinner meal out of respect for his host and as you say, him being a Lord at that."

The smile that enveloped Mary Ann's face was from paradise—an angel rejoicing—a symphony of harps—and with the beauty of the Christ Smile itself. She threw herself into a frenzy of activity half singing and half talking to no one, making preparations wherein to thank the Savior for descending in the form of the Holy Ghost who had now inspired such thoughts in her dear nephew. The name of Ledwidge was restored and heaven be praised.

## A Visit to Adare Manor

January fifteenth arrived cold but clear. All arrangements had been attended to carefully. Martin Leary, a neighbor and an old respected friend of Mary Ann and her late husband would arrive and drive Mary Ann and Francis to the depot. The train would arrive at Donegal at five o'clock if all went well.

The letter had been posted two weeks earlier to Lord Dunsany with all necessary information. Leary was prompt and the trio arrived on time at the depot.

Francis stepped into his compartment, carrying his new travel case, a gift from his aunt. Inside the case was his new Herringbone suit. An uncomfortableness overcame him. He had only spoken to Dunsany for less than a few short hours aboard ship and here he was bound into a different world than his and completely uneducated in the proper etiquette of that world. Surely Edward would see him as he was, a young fellow whose hands were destined for a plow not for knowing even the proper utensils to use for eating at the table of a Lord.

The conductor slammed all the doors closed, blew his whistle, and the train began to move. Francis stood leaning out the window waving fondly to his Aunt whose figure grew small and smaller in the distance. The rolling hills surrounded him. He closed his eyes to hear the puffing train and the click clack of wheels moving him closer and closer to his destiny.

Of the nine counties of Ulster, in Northern Ireland, Donegal is the jewel. It abounds in sweeping sandy beaches and is washed by the Atlantic Ocean. For sheer beauty of mountain, lake, valley, and peninsular coast line, Donegal is probably the most beautiful place in Ireland.

Into its Gothic station Francis' train arrived twenty minutes late. The gaslights lining the main thoroughfare and station platform were warm in their welcome. Only a few people were there to greet the passengers who were alighting from the train.

Francis, taking his gold watch from his inside vest pocket, the very one he had treasured these many years as his going to America gift from his aunt, was alarmed to see the lateness of his arrival. As he returned the watch to his pocket, a familiar voice called out in greeting.

"Francis, welcome!" Hurrying down the platform, his grey long coat flying in the chill winter wind, was himself. The warmth of Edward's greeting thawed any apprehension Francis had expected. Dunsany took his valise as if he were the servant and Francis, the master. Strange how all the proper things seemed so right in reversal!

While leading Francis down a few steps to the street level, Edward was assuring his guest that the lateness of his arrival was the fact that one could always add twenty to thirty minutes to any given arrival because the trainmen of Ireland were a unique group of men whose concerns for schedules were always superseded by the news at each station stop, and that prompt arrival meant that there was little news. Late arrival meant there was information to be digested.

Francis had forgotten! With such good humor Edward lifted the spirits of his young guest and opened to him a door through which he might not, but for Providence, have entered.

The trip to Adare Manor was a journey to remember. In passing fields, mounds of hardened turf stood huddled together for warmth. The car passed over a Roman-type bridge, under which, despite a thin crust of ice, passed a turbulent river which splashed over several levels of damlike projectors creating white, silvery foam turning from icicles—thin and spiderlike—to racing water breaking shackels of icy constraint.

Conversation was mainly about the landscape and the desolation of the roadway. Farmers had long since tended the cattle and now were sitting by their hearths inhaling the flavors from their favorite white stemmed pipes. One village they passed was shuttered and at rest despite it being early evening.

Edward, eager not to rush his friend into conversation, kept him occupied with a travelogue of the scenes they passed. Night was falling as the journey ended. The car, turning from the roadway, entered through two large gates which led to an avenue of trees which stretched to the manor house, itself a huge castlelike affair with many turrets reaching high into the night sky. The evening was clear and a myriad of shadows spread over the manor as a canopy. The bullioned windows of the main floor reflected the candlelight within.

As the touring car came to a halt in front of the entrance way, the stained glass in the upper frames of the windows cast their spectrum colors on the white limestone steps leading to the main door.

Edward, not waiting for the chauffeur to perform his duty, sprang quickly around the car, opened Francis' door, and smiled a greeting, "Welcome to my home, my boy. I hope you will enjoy your stay."

Francis overwhelmed with such a place as Adare Manor, smiled in return and said quietly, "Thank you sir, I am honored to be here."He stood looking at this magnificent castle as a tourist would while waiting in line to pay his pence for a tour of appointed rooms. He was storing in his mind the wonders of a world he had only glimpsed in those books in the library which on their silent pages reflected by the camera's eye the magnificence of lives far superior than his own.

"Shall we go inside?" Edward, as seems to be the case of those who are born to the manor, was as one greeting a friend to a humble cottage. Not that Edward was insensitive to the lad's feelings, but out of tune to the rhapsody which enveloped Francis and carried him, as if in dream, on legs which seemed not a part of himself through the door into the main hall.

Edward greeted his servant amicably and introduced his guest. He handed the portly fellow the traveling case, then maneuvered the awestruck guest towards the library which opened off of the main hall.

Need it be said that the conversation that night at dinner was constrained. Edward wondered if perhaps he should have invited Francis to the inn in the village instead. He thought now that it would have been simpler for the young man who seemed in shock with the situation in which he had been placed.

Francis sat in the velvet high-backed chair with awkwardness. Edward made up his mind to speak plainly.

"Francis lad, our conversation on board ship was so enjoyable! Friendship does not need a certain atmosphere or place to be savored. I hope you don't feel because I live in this house, or eat from china plates, or sit on baroque chairs, or sleep in a bed hung with damask draperies that I am different—not the same person with the same views as we shared on shipboard."

He looked up. Edward was sitting opposite him with his eyes searching his with kindness. His frame seemed smaller and his face older since he had seen him but a few months before. He sighed and answered, "It was the thinking about the journey and the visit that had me confused sir. Especially finding out through your letter of your position." He stammered on, "A Lord sir and me? I can't but think if I had asked you to Navan or to the home I once knew in Slane..." Here he paused.

"Would I have changed in my friendship for you because you live in a cottage? No my boy. It is quite natural that you felt this way. But now that we have put things of really so little consequence aside, let us get down to the most pleasurable part of all—your plans for the future."

From that moment on Francis and Edward resumed the conversation that had begun standing on the deck of the ship bound for Southhampton. Francis Ledwidge—farmer, and Lord Dunsany—Aristocrat.

Edward listened intently to his young friend while the latter poking a walking stick from a stand into the air punctuated his animated conversation with stabs and thrusts taking the place of exclamation marks on a student's grammar exercise!

"Politics of course interests me and the challenge of being a part for the support of a free Ireland is close to my heart. But Edward, it will take years before I can be a barrister. It is a necessary background I feel imperative to success in that endeavor."

They had risen from their chairs and taken their coats from the cloakroom and now moved outside to parklike lawns which surrounded the manor.

Edward, walking more slowly now as they approached the atrophied remnants of a large garden, nodded to a marble bench and sat down seeking rest. Francis had been talking animatedly since leaving the library a half-hour before.

"But Francis," sighed Edward, realizing the twenty three years that separated them in age, "the power of words is a gift my boy. You happen to possess it in abundance. Most probably your extensive reading, thanks in a large sense to your solitary life, has provided you with a vocabulary and style far more worthy than many members of parliament who encourage sleep rather than attention when they rise to speak in the House."

Francis pondered upon this; then resumed a vigorous response. "Edward, the university life to a large degree will add a gloss to this rough character—myself—shorn of the niceties of polite society. But to my mind I would do better to encamp in a good library and continue my independent education. I would truly like to write. I started a journal once. Remember the empty notebook my schoolmaster gave me? Well I have filled that and many more with poetry. I really hesitate to qualify them as poems. Let us say they are sentiments which at the occasion of an event of mood have translated themselves onto blank pages."

Edward with a gentle smile asked, "Do you have a journal or copybook that I might read?" Francis reddened in honest embarrassment.

"Forgive me sir. Here I sit fever pitched and carrying on as if I had some special talent that the world has been patiently awaiting. I'm ashamed of my pride and vanity. It is almost laughable if it weren't so sincere."

Edward, his face serious, continued. "There is in my mind shadows of what may be ahead for you, Francis Ledwidge. Upon your return to Navan send any or all of that which you feel has pleased you personally. Judge not harshly but honestly. I have, you know, and this may be the very fabric of our friendship, I have a love of words myself. Here I am with manor and peerage and I stand in awe of the young man I see before me. I know not what you have written but I do know the words you have spoken between us have moved me on occasions to wish I had spoken them myself!" Edward continued.

"I have written several satiric plays which disguisedly make my point concerning a free Ireland quite obvious to the erudite spectators. Yeats himself has encouraged me to present one, *Glittering Gates*, in the newly-founded Irish National Theater, the Abbey.

Francis was struck dumb. He stammered, "Sir, W. B. Yeats is producing a play by yourself in a National Theater, the Ab...." He grappled for the name.

"The Abbey Theater it will be called and it is located in Dublin."

"And me carrying on like a schoolboy with my verses. It's a wonder you could have kept a straight face during my dissertation on the joys of a boy poet."

Edward was very serious."If this theater is to survive, it must be an instrument, a voice for the Irish people, if you will who are not revolutionists with guns and tools of destruction, but voices of the Irish Republic and its culture—not its terror. This theater will be the sounding board, the arena where talented writers, poets, and singers will bring the message of Ireland to the world. It will, in my opinion, be heard by not only our countrymen but by men who seek freedom from tyranny all over the face of this earth."

"Francis, I knew this would lead to a path you were to take. This is settled in my mind. Instinct tells me the future leads you to Dublin. If God, in His mercy, has led you in this direction there is no other course but to accept it and prove worthy of that calling."

A warmth of spirit within Francis rose. It reminded him when as a lad he had lain down his school books on the road and moved to the grassy knoll and touched the silvered dew with his fingertips and known its beauty and would always know it for as long as he lived.

*I hear wing-flutters of the early birds.*
*I see the tide of morning landwind spill.*

The return trip to Navan was filled with remembrances of the conversations between the two friends. So it's Francis, writer, is it then! The train wheels repeated Abbey Theater, Yeats, Dunsany over and over again.

He had promised Dunsany to pack all his copybooks—not an easy task for nine years of work. He really had not counted them, but by now his writings filled the bottom two drawers of his room in Navan. Mary Ann—what would he tell her? Should he mention Lord Dunsany's ambitions for Francis Ledwidge of Slane?

"Keep your wits about you," he murmured to himself as the train chugged into Navan station. "Once Dunsany reads those lines of yours he may pitch them into the nearest hearthfire," he laughed aloud.

After the evening meal, that evening, he followed Mary Ann into the parlor. Both having seated themselves comfortably Francis cleared his throat and gave her a brisk review of the weekend. He gave long descriptions of the manor house and its fine adornments. To be truthful, he thought that afterward this was all Mary Ann seemed eager to hear. Discussion of poetry, although elevating was not her realm of interest!

The next morning he packed his copybooks into the large box inside which the draper had recently packaged his new herringbone suit. Upon reaching the post office the postmaster seemed uniquely interested in its contents, but Francis remaining aloof just mumbled the content as "old books". When the postage was paid there was a gasp from the postmaster who seemed to have suffered a sudden shock. "Can I help you sir?" Francis asked the white faced clerk. The old fellow pointed to the address on the box:

Lord Edward Dunsany
Adare Manor
Donegal
Ulster County
Ireland

"You'd be knowing this fellow?" stammered the postmaster looking at Francis curiously. What a choice piece of news this would be if Postmaster O'Donnell had unearthed that Francis Ledwidge and Edward Dunsany knew each other! Francis on the other hand had no need for this to become village gossip—not at this perilous moment!

"I answered an advertisement, sir which was inquiring about old textbooks. I guess this fellow Dunsany collects them. Seeing as I had a drawer full from my school days I am sending them on to him."

This explanation seemed to put the postmaster back on an even keel. He nodded and put the package on the outgoing mail table where it would begin its journey to Donegal.

One brisk March morning Francis awoke at his usual early hour, hurried through his dressing, spinning dreams as he walked down the stairs and into the parlor. He had awakened this morning with the driving compulsion to revisit Slane. He didn't know as yet if he would knock on his father's door and await whoever opened it, or whether he would just retrace his boyhood footprints over the stones across the pond and up to his fortress Ballynock. Thoughts of his father, stepmother and stepbrothers were not on his mind at all. This in a way troubled him. Of course he hadn't seen or heard directly from his father in nearly ten years. He had never met his stepmother or stepbrothers and sisters. The that concerned him most was his lack of feeling about the matter.

Mary Ann, grumbling about the chill in the air, was already in the kitchen banging pots and directed Francis to give the hearth a pat. "It's that near to extinction it is," she muttered.

Francis hurried out behind the cottage to a small shed and lifted a goodly size peat wedge and quickly returned shivering in the frosty morning air. He thought it best not to tell Mary Ann of his plans. No use raking up dead coals. He smiled.

Talk of Patrick Ledwidge had been scarce and reference to him by Mary Ann was usually only in vague terms.

"Auntie, I think today if you'll not be needing me until later. I'll be taking a walking trip to Bourne. There's a library there I haven't visited. I want to look up some things."

"If that's the case you best take the horse and trap lad. You may decide on a side trip further along. A person should be able to use a convenience when one has them, beside the horse needs some exercise as well as you, he eats enough. He might as well earn his keep. Be taking the stick by the hearth if he gives you any trouble."

The horse to which Mary Ann referred to was old Shaunassey, who, when the subject was last discussed, was estimated to be close to fourteen years of age. Good enough fellow to drive the trap to church on a bad day but truly not reliable for a journey of ten miles round trip.

"I think Shaugnassey has a severe case of gout, Auntie. I trust my two legs far more than his four."

Mary Ann pouted, "You've made your decision then lad, so be it." As Francis turned out the gate, he looked at the clear blue sky.

The quarter moon hung low on the horizon paling quickly as the sun grew stronger in the east. He drew his scarf closer around his neck as he turned the bend of the road and moved at a steady pace through the quiet village, nodding politely to one or two early shopkeepers unshuttering their shop windows.

His peaked cap shielded his blue eyes as he looked at the familiar valley leading home to Slane. Would it be changed? Had his father moved away and was the cottage still as he remembered—had it been changed in any way? Was Bugle still swishing hay into her insatiable mouth? Was Ballynock...no, never. "Never," he said aloud. Nothing could change Ballynock. Her fortress ruins have stood for centuries he reassured himself. Her crumbling turrets still housed in spring the black thorn with its sweet fragrance. The wild roses would still be huddled along her tumbled stones in small groups startling the trespasser with their delicate loveliness.

The miles passed quickly beneath his feet. With each mile a longing grew stronger and stronger as his pace grew faster. Home. Somewhere in the human heart is a place where first we were aware of love—of soft eyes, and happy times. The memories of hurt and sorrow seem to fade in recollection. The room where first our dreams are spun—the gate that welcomed us—the sounds and sights of that first home haunt us in memory all our living days. No one could ever replace those early years when each of us has awakened to self. It was as if we were travelers who found the perfect resting place but then moved on. Never again would other homes be quite the same as that first. All that came after would be compared and held to scrutiny, but never again would it be the same as that place from whence we began our life's journey.

The road turned and Francis looked up. There it was. He stood for a moment. He looked about and saw no one, yet the chimney was puffing smoke! No sign of anyone in the fields and it was noon. Could it be they were in the stable? He moved towards the gate and stopped. Those empty silent years flooded over him. The memory of a man, his father, standing on the little tender in the fog with the seagulls overhead, and then the father's letter. A terrible loneliness overwhelmed him. He swallowed the lump in his throat, turned toward the road, and started back to Navan. Never once did he turn for a fleeting glance at the cottage or his childhood fortress. Had they ever really existed he wondered.

*I strayed down a green coil of lanes where murmuring wings*
*moved up and down like lights upon the sea,*
*Searching for calm amid untroubled things of wood and water*

The weeks following his visit to Adare Manor were laden with apprehension. He felt that sending his poetry might end their relationship completely.

He muttered many times, "Imagine a playwright such as Dunsany who produces great plays for the Abbey Theatre reading my simple verses about blackbirds and meadows!"

The winter days became milder.

One morning upon waking early, Francis decided to start off for Glendalaugh, a medieval settlement a few miles down the valley. Some early wild flowers grew in patches along the dirt road. There was no one but himself to disturb the tranquil countryside at this early hour. At the turn of the road he came upon the ruins of a magnificent castle, its turrets crumbling into weathered designs. The roofless nave of the chapel lay open to the sky and clouds. What a wondrous prayer it would be for anyone who stood where once the altar stone had been placed and watched the sun rise. What beauty to see the soft rain and mist rise as incense from the sanctuary and seek its creator above the green mountains. Francis with pencil in hand wrote of this quiet place where wild hares fought their battles under the eyes of ancient warriors. Perhaps Brian Boru himself had stepped upon this very soil and knelt to receive the precious Host before mounting his horse and going to battle with the enemy. For Francis, the day ended all too soon. He put his verses in his pocket as he hurried homeward. In the darkening twilight, his thoughts once again turned to Dunsany.

He had expected to hear word from Dunsany soon after he had sent him the box of copybooks. As each week passed with no letter, he felt that his hopes had been dashed. He began to realize that there had really been only the schoolmaster who had read his boyish first rhymes long ago. The conversations with Edward were not written down and perhaps from words spoken aloud as compared to those on paper there would be a difference and that difference had not gained approval.

Arriving in Navan he hurried through the gate and saw Mary Ann looking at him from the open door. She was smiling broadly.

"It's from himself," she said proudly. Uncanny that this was the day he finally wrote, Francis thought quickly, as if I willed it. The lamp had been lit and their tea cups filled. He wanted to tear open the long awaited letter but knew his aunt would savor the contents read aloud with her tea and biscuits. The steam curled in wisps into the damp parlor air as Mary Ann settled herself as daintily as her size permitted into her chair and then nodded for him to begin.

Francis, standing near the hearth, tore open the letter and with trembling hands, opened out the three familiar folds. He skimmed the lines swiftly before he started to read aloud. He had to know. Mary Ann cleared her throat. He took up the letter.

> I shall come straight to the point. I spent an entire evening reading your poetry. I could not put one copybook down before I found myself reaching for the next. You write with simplicity. The

pastoral poetry is your best and I find you instinctively know this and write almost all of your poetry in this vein.

Your "Had I a Golden Pound" was very moving but my favorite of all was "Lament for the Poet". Your blackbirds will be remembered in the lines you've written (I have memorized them you see):

I heard the poor old woman say: At break of day the fowler came, and took my blackbirds from their songs, who loved me well through shame and blame.

*No more from lovely distances their songs shall bless me mile by mile*
*Nor to white Ashbourne call me down—*
*To wear my crown another while*
*With bended flower the angel's mark*
*For the skylark the place, They lie—*
*From there its little family*
*Shall dip their wings first in the sky*
*And when the first surprise of flight*
*Sweet songs excite and far down...*

Here Francis looked up and into his aunt's tear filled eyes and continued not looking at the letter now but saying in his own words:

*Shall there come blackbirds loud with love,*
*Sweet echoes of the singers gone.*
*But in the lonely hush of eve*
*Weeping I grieve the silent bills*
*I heard the poor old woman say*
*In Derry of the little hills.*

He looked back at the letter and continued reading

I am leaving for Dublin in a week and shall arrange accommodations that I hope will suit you. We shall settle things upon our meeting. Remember me to your much respected and devoted Aunt. Plan to stay in Dublin indefinitely.

"Plan to stay in Dublin indefinitely," spoke up Mary Ann, lulled from the mention of her in the letter to this startling news. The lad had been with her for a time now and the thought of him leaving for Dublin and for an indefinite period caused her concern.

"It's just for a short time I'm sure," said Francis not wanting to elevate his hopes and then to have them dashed. " I've got to try Auntie. Walking the countryside and writing my verses for the lantern's eye is not the life I intended if Dunsany thinks me worthy of a trip to Dublin." Mary Ann gasped.

"Dublin is it? Glory be to God, the name of Ledwidge written in a book—a book of poetry perhaps," her voice broke and she burst into tears. Why some women, when in the midst of happiness find tears their only expression confused him. This kind, warm-hearted creature was the dearest person in the world. He walked over to her. He picked up the sea conch from the mantel and placed it to her ear.

"Hear it, Auntie, the sea itself right here in the parlor!" She stopped her crying and looked at him with awe and wonder and then handed him the conch. He raised it to his ear.

"Hear the sea, Francis?" she smiled.

"No Auntie, I hear a blackbird calling."

*Shall there come blackbirds loud with love,*
*Sweet echoes of the singers gone.*
*But in the lonely hush of eve*
*Weeping I grieve the silent bills*
*I heard the poor old women say*
*In Derry of the little hills*

# Dublin

Francis Ledwidge arrived in Dublin one month after receiving Dunsany's summons. In a second brief note Dunsany directed him to a rooming house on North Circular Road. His second glimpse of Dublin stirred his imagination. His life in the greater part had been that of the pastoral nature—a meditative aura had enveloped him and to a great degree kept him a solitary figure. He had never fallen in love in his young life. Oh no, that was not true. He had been in love many times but the intensity of his passion had always died quickly. It was as if no one could sustain the flame of such devotion.

A skylark singing to the dawn, a cluster of bluebells hovering near a rusty gate, some wild roses discovered cascading over a ruined fence brought his heart and mind together and formed unconsciously and without reason a feeling not unlike awe. He saw things others would neither notice nor remember.

But what did lie ahead for the untutored farm lad? Edward Plunkett, Lord Dunsany, had found in him a young poet untainted and without a studied pose. He was to Dunsany worthy of test and trial.

North Circular Road was a district wherein many fledgling Irish writers found plain but decent lodging. His luggage was meager, his heart filled with apprehension, and his expectations in the hands of his Maker.

He arrived at the address given to him. The lodging consisted of one large room with two front casement windows overlooking a busy street. There was a fireplace with a rack for making tea and cooking a bit of stew. A long walnut table was against the wall which he immediately commandeered for his writing desk, and two gas jets on the wall, something he had never seen before.

The landlady, Mrs. O'Mara, a dour spindly woman, showed him the room with only one comment, "That'll be one month in advance, if you please." He had some of his inheritance left and planned to find a convenient banking establishment into which to deposit the sum once he had paid her the rent. He had insisted, when discussion of money had arisen with Dunsany, that he would be able to support himself for at least six months.

He handed Mrs. O'Mara her pound and six and hearing not another word from her, even a thank you, moved to close the door and encourage in that gesture, her departure. Mrs. O'Mara folding and pocketing the pound and sixpence spoke tersely, "I suppose you'll be wanting your meals?" Francis used to a frugal life saw no reason to add to his financial outlay and replied, "Thank you, no. I shall not always know the arrival or departure of myself; only fate can determine where I shall be at the evening hour." Thinking this statement would totally confuse and send her on her way, he paused.

"Sure, you're just like all those others who come and go here."

"Who?" Francis asked curiously. She put her hand on the door knob and threw her grey head back and answered with scorn," Writers!" The door slammed and rattled on its hinges. He heard his laughter fill the empty room and somehow the sound of it was a good omen!

Dublin in 1913 was alive with revolt. Street orators standing on their crates would move from corner to corner inciting passersby to action. "Free Ireland; Send the blaggards to the bottom of Liffey." The air was rife with patriotism. The bobbies did their best to move the incendiary speakers but, always if you walked down O'Connell Street a spirited voice could be heard against the street sounds, filling the air with the songs of patriots and the cry of martyrs.

Francis steeped himself with it all. He would lean against the black iron fence facing O'Connell's monument and listen to firey-faced Irishmen preach revolution. It filled him with a fierce pride for his country. It aroused deep within him a knowledge that now he might not only write of nature but of his country with passion.

He had not met with Dunsany the first week of his arrival. He knew that he was completing his manuscript *The Glittering Gates*, a satiric play concerning the political scene and that it was soon to be presented at the Abbey Theatre. Thinking about it overwhelmed him. He had chosen a path indeed which brought him to the very heights that dreams might allow. He would in those first weeks, while waiting for the kettle to boil, dwell on how remarkable it was that he had come to know Edward Plunkett Dunsany, a friend, an inspiration, and a patron by an act of fate!

*The moon leans on one silver horn*
*Above the silhouettes of morn,*
*And from a nest—sills finches whistle*
*Or stooping pluck the downy thistle.*

## The Abbey Theatre

The newly founded Abbey Theatre was in truth a small theater. The galleries rose steeply to an arched ceiling. One had the sensation when looking down upon the stage that he was hovering just above the scenery and the actors and if he moved too closely to the edge of his seat, he would topple into the scene itself.

Francis often sat in the high gallery. There were three. He marveled at the movement and the passion beneath him. W. B. Yeats' play *The Hour Glass*, was rehearsing with the great O'Casey himself producing it. Frequently O'Casey would sit in one of the stalls (a boxlike affair close to the stage), and hum in satisfaction, or on occasion clear his throat which signalled the actor under scrutiny to tune up his performance. Francis had not been introduced to O'Casey but he felt he understood the pixie-faced playwright. He thought it interesting that the bespeckled writer was able to portray in his characters such sadness and despair within the souls of those who give their sons to the sea.

Dunsany encouraged Francis to become a permanent fixture in the theatre to absorb the plays and the actors interaction with written words thus expanding his own horizons.

Dunsany had in every way made it known to him that he was his patron. He was the one who opened doors for young talent.

Francis and Dunsany, as he now always referred to him—omitting the Lord not out of disrespect, but because Dunsany himself had insisted upon it—spent evenings in the library and long leisurely days walking the paths in the manor's grounds.

One morning after breakfast Dunsany, having read Francis' verses most of the night, laid the copybook on the table and said seriously,

"I've read many of your verses in this past year and a half of our friendship. I've edited some but not as to take the spirit from them—those that move me greatest should be published."

Francis looked up and said quietly: "I don't think they are good enough, sir."

"Why do you think I have given you these past experiences in Dublin and here in the manor lad, if it was not to have your work brought to the attention of the public?"

"Imagine a grown man such as I writing in a ten pence copybook and storing it in chest drawers. My father would find a laugh in that." That was the first time he had ever brought his father into a conversation but there it was. He still lived within the son.

"There are those lad," Dunsany interrupted, "who do not see the stars but only the darkness which is night. There are many who standing in the midst of beauty seem not aware of its presence. Blame them not Francis. It is not given to many to see as you do. Only by reading your verses will some of them understand. I believe the time is now. I shall contact an agent on Market Street upon our return next week to Dublin. Let us have his opinion on the matter."

Francis looked at Dunsany and said, "Sir, without you I would have been in darkness: I would have had no star to light the night of my mind."

## The Return to Navan

The last days of August were sultry. Rain sudden and torrential at times confined Francis to his room in Dublin. Dunsany was deeply involved at the manor with Yeats who was to produce *The Glittering Gates* at the Abbey in the fall repertory.

No word had been received from the agent on Market Street as to the prospect of publishing the verses which Dunsany admired so much. Francis depressed by the unending bad weather decided one morning to visit Mary Ann. He could catch the train and be in Navan by nightfall. Leaving a note for Dunsany with his landlady, Mrs. O'Mara, he arrived at the station in time to purchase his ticket and make the train with seconds to spare.

A trip such as this, unexpected and on a lark, improved his disposition. Once on the train to Navan he felt as a schoolboy on holiday. The purple twilight faintly pierced by newly arriving stars deepened, and as the train arrived at Navan station Francis spied the familiar figure of Fergus McNaught, the stationmaster.

"Ledwidge, you're a sight to behold. And how is dear old Dublin?" Francis had asked Mary Ann not to reveal any of his business in Dublin to anyone. He was relieved that Mary Ann had restrained herself and avoided any temptation to divulge information about his activities.

"Back for good, lad?" asked McNaught.

"Just for a few days visit sir, replied Francis with a friendly grin.

Then you've not be knowing the news then."

Francis' heart stopped for a moment. "News?"

McNaught putting his arm around Francis' shoulder moved him towards the inside of the platform. "You're not knowing about your father's wife?"

Francis breathed again." No, I do not sir."

"Well," McNaught heaved a sigh and proceeded to give him the news that at this moment was inside a letter which Mary Ann had posted four days before and which now was on the hall table at Mrs. O'Mara's awaiting his return."It seems your father, Patrick, a fine broth of a man whom I may say, I haven't seen here in many a year, arrived on horseback a fortnight ago..."

Francis, relieved that Mary Ann was among the living and his father also, sighed and moved to a bench nearby. McNaught continued.

"Well now, we found out later after your father had come into Navan, from Martin O'Leary, your aunt's old friend, that Patrick's woman died in childbirth. A baby girl died with her. Mary Ann went of course to do what she could. Now isn't it strange that yourself arrived by chance today! Tis strange and mysterious it tis."

At this point McNaught shaking his whitened head placed a finger to his cheek and repeated several times the phrase: "A power higher than us all moves in strange ways." When McNaught looked down at the bench, Francis was gone.

He moved swiftly down the main road towards Mary Ann's little cottage. She was still in Slane no doubt. He expected the house to be dark but no, the familiar lamplight was lit. He pushed open the gate, knocked on the door as was always his custom before entering, and waited for the footsteps which were sure to follow. The door opened cautiously and the figure grasped the lad to her—her dear Francis.

"Francis, how did you know?" She released him taking his arm and leading him to his chair.

"McNaught told me when I arrived, Auntie." She took his valise and placed it by the stairs.

"You look pale, lad. There is so much to ask and to tell you. I wrote you, but I see the letter and you never met. Rest lad. I'll pour us a cup of tea before starting supper." She moved into the kitchen, skirts rustling familiarly. He looked about and realized he had missed the place and Mary Ann more than he had known. It was home.

They sat together long into the night sharing each other's news. "Sure Patrick was indeed a stranger," Mary Ann mused. "Never heard a thing about him since you came home almost two years now. I used to write now and again, but in all the years there may have been three letters between us. I heard the place has had hard times and that he was a stern task master to the woman and three boys."

Francis listened as if detached. He wondered if any of the three had fallen short in their duties or caused his father heartache because of book-learning. "Did any of them go to the National School, Mary Ann?"

"That I don't know lad. If your father had the last word I'm sure they learned their lessons in the stable or clearing the fields. The woman was not liked. Tis a puzzle to know how those two cold fish could stand each other," Mary Ann smiled. "Deserved each other I'd say." She looked at Francis' face. He seemed not to be listening.

"Would you like to be paying a visit to Slane? I'd be glad to accompany you if you'd be wanting me along?"

He looked up startled by the directness of her question. It had not crossed his mind to retrace those steps he had taken but a short time ago.

"No, but thank you Mary Ann. I'll not be going that way again." Seeing he had dismissed the idea already she rose and went to start the supper. He stared through the window into the growing darkness. A partial new moon hung at the top of the window. No star accompanied it. It stood solemn and alone gazing down at him. He would stay for a few days with his aunt and perhaps go down the valley to Ardon Mor which rose to a sloping hill overlooking an inlet wherein herons conversed and sang sweet songs. He needed to cleanse the bitterness which the news had brought to him. A reminder that time and circumstances hadn't changed the nature that his father possessed.

The next morning he started down the path which wound by Balbriggan where sprays of wild daisies entwined themselves between fences and styles. Passing through the moor he came upon the shore of Sheelin Lake. He stood looking down upon a troupe of herons gossiping. He took his copybook and sat upon a flat stone and wrote:

*As I was climbing Ardon Mor*
*From the shore of Sheelin Lake*
*I met the herons coming down*
*Before the water's wake*
*And they were talking in their flight*
*Of dreamy ways the herons go*
*When all the hills are withered up*
*Nor any water flow...* The pencil *stopped—*

The day had passed so quickly he thought he'd finish the poem tomorrow, or perhaps that was all he had to say of such a moment upon which he had intruded. For the rest of the afternoon Ledwidge walked about the moor listening to the songs of the thrush and linnet. Once the high, haunting note of the blackbird sitting on a branch in the alder tree caused him to turn and gaze upon that solitary singer.

The sky was turning violet and pink as his gaze returned to the alder tree. The singer had fled and so too had the afternoon.

His visit to Mary Ann had refreshed him. He had wandered about the countryside pausing to jot down impressions until his legs had given out. He had resumed his insatiable thirst for new sights and sounds which would be stored away in memory and later put together in yet another verse!

The day of his departure was settled upon and on his last evening he sat with Mary Ann before the hearth. She seemed depressed, as indeed she was, having enjoyed the looking after of her nephew. She savored the talks they had. " You won't be staying a few days longer?"

Francis smiled. "It's hard to resist the offer Auntie, but I must get back and find out about this verse making. I've got to get some word about the verses I'll be making, or I may have to apprentice myself to the local draper to earn a livelihood."

"What's this?" Mary Ann rose in shock. "To be a draper is it? You the maker of pictures in the mind. You have only to see the tears that I couldn't hold back with the beauty of those poems you read me. Nonsense! The devil take that old book agent. You lad, have been touched by the hand of God." She sputtered—running out of words as she groped now to find a way to reveal how important writing should be to him.

Francis rose to his feet to calm the poor soul. "Auntie, you have given me a new resolve! I might have put a rejection by one literary agent as the sole criteria for my writing." Mary Ann nodded, "You're a clever lad who listens to his old aunt. Many a song I've sung since I was a colleen, but never have the words I've sung seemed so sweet as those you make."

"If ever there was one who lifted me from the lack of faith in myself it is you dear aunt." Mary Ann looked at him with the twinkle returning to her wide blue eyes.

Before Francis fell asleep that night he felt a peace that was new to him. He didn't hear his door open quietly or see his aunt standing by the foot of his bed.

So sound was his sleep he never heard her words:

"Sure isn't it a wonder to have such a lad as he and him telling me I was a treasure close to his heart. Me life has some meaning after all."

The stars grew bright over the little cottage reflecting the happiness that dwelt there within, where the two sleepers with contented hearts slumbered through the hours toward a new dawn.

## Ellie Vaughey

Francis arrived back in Dublin refreshed. He had completed the poem 'Ardan Mor.' He met Dunsany at O'Rourke's, an eating place off Market Street, the haunt of many writers, playwrights, musicians, and politicians. Sitting next to Dunsany who stood and shook his hand warmly as he came to the table was a childlike young woman who kept her eyes down on the plate of sausages she was eating.

"Here's the lad now, Ellie. See how his cheeks are ruddied by the country air he's been basking in no doubt this fortnight."

Francis shook Dunsany's hand. "Good to be back sir."

"My boy, this is Ellie—Ellie Vaughey, a singer of songs." The young woman looked up at Francis. The eyes were violet and fringed with thick black lashes. They had a sadness that startled him. He looked down upon her intently. "Are you from Dublin Miss Vaughey?" " Sit down lad," Dunsany said pulling up a chair from the adjoining table and motioning him to take a place at the girl's side.

Ellie looked at Francis and then down at her plate again. Lifting her fork to resume her lunch she replied in a low voice. "I'm from Glendalagh, Mr. Ledwidge". The waiter thinking Francis a new patron hurried over and presented him with the bill of fare. Then taking a second look he remarked, "Your usual sir?" Francis was pleased. He and Dunsany regularly frequented O'Rourke's. He replied off handedly,

"The usual." The usual was either grilled salmon or roast chicken on a slice of ham. The waiter, remembering Ledwidge's two favorite dishes, decided that the salmon was exceptionally palatable today and made for the kitchen. Dunsany spent the remainder of the luncheon regaling the two young people with news of the Abbey, the production schedule for the fall, and the laborious frantic time he was having preparing his play.

Francis took furtive glances at Miss Vaughey studying her with care. She was about twenty, with dark hair with a soft wave worn smoothly against her small head. She seemed to be quite petite. Her cheeks were of high color and her lips full and expressive. She smiled often at Dunsany's monologue with teeth white and even. Most country girls Francis had met had stained teeth or one or more missing. He had forgotten the burning question that had plagued him since he sought escape at Navan. What about the book agent and his verses?

Dunsany rambled on. The salmon arrived and was finished when Dunsany at last cleared his throat, fell silent, then with a roar of laughter looked at the two seated next to him. "My God, I have been a bore ranting on and on and never once letting either of you get a word in. Ellie, I have a favor to ask. I see that Morgan Leary has come in and brought his Guinness to the piano which means we are about to be treated to some lively tunes. What say you, dear girl, to sing a favorite tune of mine—The Rose of Tralee?"

Ellie paled and her lips quivered slightly. "Here, sir?" She could barely be heard.

"Why of course, Miss Vaughey, everyone here is quite friendly. We don't at the moment have another lovely one as you to sing such a sweet tune," encouraged Dunsany.

Francis smiled at her. "I'd be pleased if you would too, Miss Vaughey."

Her eyes lingered on him as if to gain strength. She rose gracefully with Francis holding out her chair and Dunsany leading her slight form toward the piano.

Morgan Leary paused to sip his stout, smiled broadly, and played a sweeping adagio asked, "What will it be darlin?"

"The Rose of Tralee in C," she sighed. The patrons of O'Rourke's had thinned as the lunch hour passed. Only a few remained. They quieted as she stood beside the piano with one hand lightly touching it as if for balance.

The loveliness of her voice was touching. The youthfulness of her mingled with the lyrics had captivated the listeners. Silence greeted her final note. Her eyes were filled with tears. The listeners stood now to a person clapping and calling, "Encore!" They surged about her, aware that her presence had the aura of a special occasion. Her eyes fell upon Francis who had been pushed back by the group. The look between them shone for all to see, but only the two of them knew of it.

Walking home to his flat that September evening, Francis found himself in turmoil. The doleful eyes of Ellie haunted him. This newly discovered emotion within him caused him to pause by a small iron gate leading into a parklike area recessed from the street. He pushed open the rusting aperture and entered what seemed to be an ancient cemetery whose headstones leaned forward and backward in strange postures. The dates here and there gave testimony to the time these forgotten creatures had walked upon the earth.

Oh God, how pathetic we are. Vanity riding upon our shoulders, smiling unto itself in our hopeless journey into age. Shaking himself and closing the gate behind him he wondered at the mind which in one moment could be caught up in love and then within a turn of the road could come face to face with eternity.

As he let himself into the flat and lit the gas lamps his thoughts moved to a concern which until now seemingly lay forgotten. No doubt Dunsany had set the stage for this afternoon's diversion. The agent had probably told Dunsany of the hopelessness of his verse and his patron meant to soften the news with an afternoon at O'Rourke's and the presentation of a new protege, Miss Vaughey.

Francis flung his coat on the cot and crossed to the fireplace, and with heavy heart prepared the hearth providing the only warmth which now could occupy his spirit. Having concluded these ministrations, he sank dejectedly into his chair and attempted to close out those sad violet eyes and that sweet voice which now filled his soul.

A loud insistent rapping at this door roused him from a deep and dreamless sleep. Startled to find himself slumped in the chair he looked at the blackened and shrunken log in the fireplace under which whitened ashes testified to the length of time he had been asleep. The gas lamps sputtered against the brilliance of a new sun which splashed across the faded wallpaper.

"Good Lord, what time can it be?"

He rose and moved towards the persistent knocking. Pushing back the latch he threw open the door and saw Dunsany standing impatiently waiting to come in.

"The sleep of the angels, lad. That's what comes of a sinless conscience, a hearty meal, and the vision of a lovely girl—talented too."

Francis stared as Dunsany burst through the door with a swish of his cape, tossed his cane on the bed, and placed a package on the chair so recently vacated by its sleeping occupant.

"Open it, lad and be quick about it. We have many things to settle this day."

Francis closed the still opened door, moved to the chair, and proceeded to follow Dunsany's directions. Dunsany, in the meantime, walked to the window keeping his back to Francis as he unwrapped the package.

How many minutes in the day and years of our earthly presence can we hold a full measure of happiness—complete and untainted by the hint of worry or conscience or sadness stealing in upon that perfect time and putting shadows across its brilliance? Such was an occasion in the life of Francis Ledwidge. For when the wrapping fell from the object in his hands, the joy that rose within him was never to be found or discovered in such perfection again.

There in his hands lay himself! The cover read: "The Songs of the Blackbird" by Francis Ledwidge. Turning the pages and speaking softly to himself he read the titles of his verses. The print dissolved into the fortress of Ballynock, the herons and sandpipers at Sheelin Lake, and the fragrance of the flowers that grew by the strand... "And when the first surprise of flight sweet songs excites, and from far down shall there come the blackbirds loud with love, sweet echoes of the singers gone." His voice broke; he slumped into the chair. Tears of joy and pain filled his eyes and his soul rejoiced. The maker of verses had now a voice for others to hear. Perhaps they too would find a song within that book they too could sing.

Dunsany's judgment was acute. He, from the beginning, had trusted his instinct. Francis was a gifted lad not destined for the plough but for the pen. The book agent had interested the largest publishing house, Peers, in publishing the collection of Ledwidge's poetry limiting the edition to a conservative one thousand copies. It was Dunsany who devised the plan to allow the public to hear the verses from the poet himself!

## The Abbey

On a wintry March evening before the red velvet curtain of the Abbey Theatre and the opening of Dunsany's play, *Glittering Gates*, Lord Edward John Drax Plunkett walked across the apron of the stage and holding up one hand to quiet the audience spoke in the manner of a schoolmaster giving an introduction to one of the student body about to deliver a valedictory which was in a sense quite appropriate for the occasion.

"Ladies and Gentlemen, before you see and hear *Glittering Gates* I should like you to meet The Abbey's newest discovery—a young man from Slane (here several hurrahs from the galleries). Perhaps, " Dunsany smiled acknowledging the Slane supporters, "Perhaps you know the lad already, a writer of verse which shall touch the hearts of you all. May I now present Francis Ledwidge." With that Dunsany turned and nodded to Francis who stood perspiring profusely in the wings dabbing a handkerchief to his deathlike forehead.

He walked slowly through the scattered applause, sensing the audience's impatience to be burdened with a tiresome poet. Reaching Dunsany's side with head bent daring not to raise his eyes to the audience, Ledwidge lifted the thin volume and turned the pages to the poem, "Had I A Golden Pound." Dunsany walked quickly from the stage and took his place on a stool in the rear of the stage.

Francis' voice thin and tremulous lent itself to the sadness of the verse.

There are special moments between a performer and an audience wherein both are givers and receivers; each sustaining the other in a completeness that has to be experienced to be understood. Such were those minutes which the Abbey audience evening would always remember and say, "That evening when young Ledwidge, the pale poet of Slane, read his poetry was a special time that I shall always remember."

The weeks following were busy for Francis. He had seen Ellie once more at a Sunday concert at Gilabe Hall, an ancient and historic place, that presented musical talent to audiences. He had heard from Dunsany that she would be appearing with a harpist as her accompanist.

The afternoon of her performance was grey and the sky threatened snow. Francis joined the small audience sitting himself well to the back hidden to a degree by a pillar. He hadn't seen her in weeks and wondered if his awareness of her which followed her singing in O'Rourke's was as important to her as it was to him.

The stage was elevated only slightly from the floor and Francis could barely see the top of her head as she entered from a small door in the back of the stage. The harpist, a redheaded rosy cheeked youth, plucked several chords to carry her to the center of the platform. As there were no programs, she began to introduce her first song in a voice resolute and spirited.

"I should like to begin with Thomas More's, The Minstral Boy." She nodded to the harpist, then moved to the very edge of the platform nearest the audience. As the song moved to the height of the lyric her voice soared and then broke as a fragile crystal shattering. The note fell in clusters and the audience watched painfully. She then walked towards the harp and plucked the string of the high note that had shattered in her first rendition. Francis stood and looked to see if he could leave as not to be noticed, so heavy hearted and saddened was he at what had happened. Then the high note sung alone pierced his soul. She had started again at the very place her voice had faultered. "No faithful song will praise thee…" She completed the song as no one else would or could have done. The audience now stood and cheered. She had deliberately broken on that note! Of course, what genius! At the very part where the warrior dies, yet the songs he sings live on. The harp plays on.

Francis, astounded at the magic she had created, was caught up in the fervor as was the audience. Had she rescued herself from disaster with such finesse? Was it part of her performance?

The afternoon was a triumph! The small but enthusiastic audience moving from the hall into the snow spoke to each other with comraderie and all to a person felt they had been present to the discovery of another great talent. Francis folding his coat over his arm, made his way to the little door at the back of the stage. He knocked and waited. The door was opened by the red cheeked harpist. Miss Vaughey, Ellie, appeared with her long blue woolen coat wearing a cloche and pulling on a pair of red mittens.

"Mr. Ledwidge, what a nice gesture. I saw you at the beginning of the program. I'm so glad you decided to stay to the end." He blushed. She had seen his attempt at an early departure.

"Are you getting a taxi home or shall we walk in this marvelous weather?" He looked into those clear violet eyes and smiled broadly. "Miss Vaughey, a day such as this is to be savored." And into the snowfall they walked turning a corner and laughing, leaving their footprints but for a minute behind them.

"Her laughter will ring far, and I will call her names of flowers"

## The Tea Shop

On a late summer afternoon Francis walked Gregory Street looking down at the top of his brown brogans. Tiny particles of dust had caught the waning sun which threw darts of light on the sidewalk. The last thing in the world was to consider giving the boots a polish. He smiled. "With all around me girding their lives for battle, I walk down a street caught up with the beauty of dusty boots."

"Are you avoiding me Francis Ledwidge?" The lilting voice shook him from his reverie. There facing him was Ellie. Her eyes appraised him swiftly. She looked so beautiful. Her hair was neatly tucked into a chignon type of lace at the nape of her neck and her pale blue dress set off the violet color of her expressive eyes.

"What a pleasant surprise Ellie," he swallowed hard.

"I've asked about for you at O'Rourke's and Tunney's and heard you were very busy with recitals in and about Dublin."

"I haven't seen you, Francis, since that snowy afternoon when we walked for miles it seemed and then found a little tea shop off Dunstan Road! Remember the old lady with the false curls that dipped into her teacup each time she sipped? We had a wonderful chat. I've missed you!"

"Can we go back?" He smiled broadly. He had missed her too. Somehow she had never quite left his mind despite his lately depressing state and the disappointment at the lack of sales of his poetry.

Nan's inheritance was now almost gone. He'd soon be hunting for a position. Perhaps the specter of life as a draper that he had once laughed about would soon be a reality. But for now Ellie's presence and the warmth and scent of lilac in the gardens along the road lifted his spirits.

Ellie put her arm lightly through his, caught her slim fingers about his hand. They made an abrupt stop turning south towards Dunstan Road and the teashop. The two figures, one tall and pale and the other small and dainty, made a handsome couple to passersby, who smiled to themselves remembering walks of their own. They made their way to the teashop and arrived in time to see their talisman, a stooped and bewigged old lady opening the door to the merry accompaniment of a little bell poised over the entrance. Ellie looked at Francis with devilment in her eyes. "I do believe she shall be our good luck charm Mr. Ledwidge, it's herself and on time at that. It must be exactly four fifteen!" As they made their way to a window facing the small back garden, they heard the quarter past the hour strike on the clock behind the front counter where the elderly owner sat keeping the day's receipts under her close surveillance.

Francis looked up. Indeed right to the minute. They both laughed and seated themselves. Having ordered scones and a pot of tea they settled down comfortably to a conversation which concerned itself with each other's activities since they had last met.

"I've really meant to ask you Ellie but I thought you might find me insensitive," he stammered.

"About the recital and the high note where my voice broke?" Ellie interrupted without hesitation..."yes, yes, quite effective I would say. The audience could talk of nothing else." He gazed into her dancing eyes. Was she laughing at him, he wondered? Was it a brilliant recoup after a disastrous blunder?

She looked at him and the merriment disappeared and a sadness overcame her. "My voice did indeed break Francis. I just gathered myself together and tried again—all bravado. Thank God the same audience didn't attend my next recital where I sang the Minstrel Boy without the melodramatics." She looked down at her teacup sighing deeply.

"The career of Ellie Vaughey has ended. I'm so glad Lord Dunsany never really encouraged me to take it seriously."

"What are you doing now?" He was startled at this disclosure and yet relieved for what reason he couldn't truly understand at the moment and became silent.

"I have been employed, thanks to Lord Dunsany's kindness at St. Timothy's School, teaching vocal music to a group of delightful children ages twelve to fifteen. We are preparing for a Term End Chorale and"...she paused, her cheeks flaming "and Francis, I do love it!"

She smiled. She did look radiant. Had he envisioned her as one destined for fame in the recital halls of Cork or the Opera society in Dublin? Her fame and his position as an unknown poet seemed always to have cast a shadow over his dreams for her. He reached out and took her small hand into his. "You're looking at Dunsany's folly, Ellie. My poetry books are gathering dust in the book shops and my friends are almost gone. Do you think Dunsany might find me a place, perhaps as a teacher of English at St. Timothy's?"

Having said it he felt stupid. Would she think that he considered her a failure? He started to pull his hand from hers. She must have known how she sensed his bumbling for she reached her other hand and closed both over his saying, "Francis, you have a gift. I have a pleasant voice but not a great voice. Therein is a world of difference. No classroom could contain your soaring spirit, dearest."

He looked at her. Sitting there before him the afternoon sun filtering through the little panes of glass illuminated her in a golden light—he said softly, "I love you Ellie." He spoke with tenderness. She looked up and her eyes filled with tears. "I love you too Francis."

The clock struck the hour. The proprietress patted her calico cat sitting on the counter top as Francis laid the six pence before her. The little bell rejoiced as the door closed behind them.

*"I feel that she will come in blue with two curls strayed out of her comb's loose stocks and shall steal behind and lay my hands upon her eyes. Look not, but be my Psyche! Her laughter will ring far, as she tries for freedom I will call her names of flowers, and in the blue of hiding violets, watching for her face listening for her in every dusky place—"*

## St. Timothy's

St. Timothy's School on Highgrove Street was an impressive greystone building which stood next to a small church and rectory for nearly seventy years.

Its belfry was alive with starlings, who paused to alight on its thin pinnacled roof, in their flights to and from Dublin and its outlying villages. Only when the bell was rung by the Reverend Maurice O'Mahon, did they flee from the sonorous and powerful call to matins and mass.

Francis, pausing to look up at the parochial scene, muttered genially, "A pleasant place for Ellie to teach music." The brisk autumn breeze caught some dry scarlet leaves and sent them whirling into the bright sun above. Walking quickly towards the school entrance, Francis notices the Reverend O'Mahon ahead of him turning onto the path. The priest, whitened head downward, mounted the steps of the churchwith care.

"Father O'Mahon" is it? Francis called to the preoccupied Pastor. The good priest lifted the black skirts of his alb and continued climbing the high-pitched stairs tucking the robe under each arm as he maneuvered towards the entrance.

"Father O'Mahon." This time Francis lifted his voice louder.

The figure stood quite still, then turned back and looked quizzically at him with a startled expression on his wrinkled face.

"You be calling to me lad; can I be of help to you?" He looked like an ancient gnome with the wisdom of the ages lying within those piercing dark eyes.

"Father I've come to see Ellie Vaughey, a friend." He got no further. The priest took him briskly by the arm and did an abrupt rightface, then toddled towards the Church. "Sure and you've come a little before the practice hour my boy. You'll have time to visit with your friend before the children come."

The pastor ushered a smiling Ledwidge inside the flickering shadowed church, opened a door in the back wall, and puffing heavily led Francis up the narrow stairs to the choir loft above.

A young boy, wondering what the racket was stood at the top of the stairs. Seeing the Pastor, he smiled broadly, "Good afternoon Father." This young fellow was the pumper, without whose strong arms, the notes from the mighty organ would never have been translated from wind to music!

As Father O'Mahon reached the choir loft proper, he leaned his frame wearily against a long pewlike bench. Francis, seeing Ellie seated at the organ, moved quickly past the priest and grasped her hands. The two, lost in each others eyes, were drawn apart by the sound of muffled voices and footsteps approaching for choir practice.

"I was passing by, Ellie, and I had to know about how you were getting on. May I wait for you? Can we have supper together?" Her eyes were bright and luminous.

"I won't be subjecting you to practice Francis, she said quietly, but I'll be finished in an hour, and shall meet you at Tunney's." Francis withdrew his clasp from the long slender fingers.

"I'll have a table waiting for you," he whispered. The children, taking their places, nodded to the pastor and said as in one voice, Good afternoon Father. Then looking from Ellie to Ledwidge with knowing smiles said, "Good afternoon Miss Vaughey."

Ellie placed her fingers on her lips and spoke to the children with authority, "We shall begin now with the alto section this afternoon. We need to strengthen those lower notes in our performance of the cantata."

Father O'Mahon led Francis back down the stairs and into the Church proper.

"Would you be a Catholic, lad?" he asked Francis with a wry smile.

"I am." The old priest dipped his fingers into the holy water and splashed himself ceremoniously. There was a lilt in his step as he left the church which seemed to convey his approval of Ledwidge. He chuckled, quietly pleased, that this clerical lephrachaun would find such great pleasure in such a small coincidence of faith!

The pastor shook his hand with enthusiasm and turning again towards the school said over his shoulder, "I have a feeling lad I'll be seeing yourself here quite frequently. Sure if you're looking for companionship while waiting for Miss Vaughey, you've only to knock on the rectory door. Meself is never far from St. Timothy's." Francis nodded and smiled.

"Never far from St. Timothy's," the words echoed in his head as he turned down the street towards Tunney's.

"The man has found his place. No truer words of faith had he spoken." Francis mused aloud, "He has found a place wherein to serve and find contentment; a piece of the earth on which to spend his lifetime laboring in the cause of others."

"How many of those weary faces I meet so often in the street, or trams who grind out their days with no brightness in their eyes or smiles to ease their lonely existence."

How many such as Father O'Mahon who kneel in their chapel illuminated in the flickering shadows offer prayers for the desperate and for those who have lost all hope. Who, but this priest and all priests who in the robes of the Church's nobility, keep reminding the stray lambs of the relentless love that abounds in the Christman who seeks us all!

Francis sighed and pulled his jacket yet closer to him. He took out his father's watch at the corner of Daine and Great High Street. "My God, I've walked further than I thought," he said to himself. He turned toward Hollis Street which stretched before him and hastened his steps realizing that he might miss Ellie when she alighted from the tram which stopped directly in front of the restaurant.

The sun had lost its brightness and clouds were gathering. He had determined in these past few weeks to ask Ellie to marry him. He knew that he would never find one that meant as much to him as she.

Thoughts swept over him. Who is to speak of love and find an answer?—To reach out into the vastness of our excursion through life and select one—one with whom to walk the rest of the road in harmony and peace is almost an act of the supernatural! In simpler times, marriage was not as perilous. Love puts passion to the test as the body ages and the beauty of soul is all that remains to remind us of the promise we made at the altar of our youth! Our faith—my God—Faith. What is faith? What but a song sung by the believers from the verses of two thousand years.

He leaned against a lamp post. He wanted only to ask Ellie to marry him and now he was deep within a self-inquiry of himself and his love of Ellie. He heard the tramcar and saw the firesparks from its wheels as it turned the corner into Hollis Street. He moved quickly towards Tunney's.

In after years, he went over and over what happened in those next minutes with the clinical analysis of the devoted technician and yet he never could look at his analysis without the tears streaming down his cheeks.

He reached Tunney's and was looking at the tram coming to a stop when a man moved from the corner of a dry good shop, directly opposite the restaurant as if to catch the tram when it came to a halt. He was aware of only two people coming towards the exit of the car to alight. It was Ellie and another passenger whom he never looked at.

Ellie, seeing Francis, smiled and waved her hand. The door of the tram opened and explosions tore into the late afternoon. Francis saw her pause and turn back as if to hide, and then another round of explosions ripped the stillness, and she tumbled down the steps to the ground, her arms reaching out for shelter. Reason gone, he ran towards her. The loud sharp sounds continued. A man fell next to Ellie. The tram door slammed and it moved forward. Patrons of Tunney's poured into the street. Ledwidge could hear the sound of the assassin's boots running down the alley and the hushed voices of people whispering. "It's an Informer."

A young boy, with his dark hair lay spread askew on the cobblestones, his cap lying in the gutter, and a large red hole in the left side of his head lay dead upon Hollis Street.

Francis placed his finger's on Ellie's silken lids and closed those questioning eyes as he held her close to his heart. He had lost her!

## The Bridal Bouquet

The cemetery at St. Michael's, in Glendalough, was filled with the family and friends of Ellie Vaughey. The bright spirit that was she lay still and waxen inside the plain brown coffin. A spray of wild roses—her bridal bouquet, Francis said, lay on top of her casket.

Father Maurice O'Mahon, dressed in his white surplice stood in the grey of the morning looking shrunken and with eyes so reddened that his voice broke now and again as he read the service for the Dead.

Ledwidge who still couldn't believe what had happened as final, stood with Ellie's mother and father. Dunsany stood behind them with all the villagers and the children from St. Timothy's.

There suddenly arose over this sad place, a fierce wind that bent the trees and caused the mourners to clutch coats and hats. Father O'Mahon braced himself against the fury, blessed her grave, and turned to the mourners speaking in short gasps.

"Ellie Vaughey is at peace, dear friends. The trouble of our land has again touched the innocent. This lovely woman has joined the martyrs whose blood also was spilled without meaning—no cause other than love of God and of her fellow man was the purpose of her brief life. She will remain in our hearts always." The pastor of St. Michael's, fearing another funeral, hurried over to Father O'Mahon and placed a topcoat over his shoulders.

The two priests walked over to the Vaughey's offering their condolences and then to Ledwidge. Dunsany at this moment stepped up beside Francis and led him to the wooden gate that opened to the road and the car he had hired. The group moved slowly from the grave and past Francis and Dunsany toward the Vaughey farmhouse not far from the cemetery. Francis turned to Dunsany. "Go on sir, I'd like to stay awhile. It's too soon for her to be alone." Dunsany got into the car and nodded to the driver to move on. Mr. Vaughey touched Francis' shoulder as he passed and murmured, "You're welcome lad to have some tea and fruitcake the missus has prepared." The broken hearted man stopped, tears streaming down his face, and hurried after the retreating group down the lane.

Francis, hatless and his great coat flapping in the wind, turned back to see the men lowering the casket into the earth with long ropes. The pain in his throat stifled him. He walked slowly towards the grave seeing the roses bravely clinging to the coffin. One of the men said to Ledwidge, "Would you be wanting of the flowers sir?"

He moved forward. "I would." The man reached down and pulled a rose free from the bouquet and handed it to him. "Thank you. It was kind of you," his voice broke. He turned and walked from the place. He could hear the shovels scraping and would remember their sound forever.

"The light of one fair face that pain would stay upon the heart's broad canvas."

A month after Ellie died Francis returned to Navan to visit Mary Ann. She, who had never met Ellie, knew how much he had loved the girl. It was in his letters and in his eyes whenever he had spoken of her. She asked little only to inquire of him if he might want to call upon the Vaughey's before he returned to Dublin.

"No, I don't really know them Auntie," he said. "I think in a way they may blame me for her death."

"Impossible," Mary Ann retorted hotly. "It was the fates, Francis."

"The fates indeed," sighed Francis, Mary Ann went on quickly.

"I've lived longer than you, Francis, and in what I've seen of life, I know we have precious little to do with what happens for good or evil."

Francis looked at the plump figure before him with interest.

"Why I could tell you many a story of this very village where the fates managed to turn lives upside down, and in other cases put things right which no one could find an answer for except to put it down to the intervention or benevolence of God Himself."

"Then, the fates, as you call them, are marauding angels who sweep over the chimney tops and down the village street raising their swords in vengeance indiscriminately" he spat out the words in anger.

Mary Ann, seeing his mood, rose and turned her attention quickly to another matter. "Did you know that Martin Daugherty has a plaque in the Corgingham Arms Hotel with some of your verses on it? Did you go to Slane at all this past year with me without knowing? Sure you're a famous man now."

"I imagine there are now crowds surging around Daugherty's hotel reading those verses and heralding a major poet for Ireland." He laughed aloud. "I say they are more likely buying another Guinness Stout as they read aloud the stanzas. No, Auntie, I haven't been to Slane for a long time." His voice dropped to a whisper, "Believe the last time was when my stepmother died and I got as far as my own front door."

Mary Ann, seeing her attempt to ease his despair floundering, lifted her broad taffeta skirts and swept by him up the stairs. "I can see your tune is bitter lad so let us cease our, our…" she stumbled for words.

He walked quickly to the dearest one left to him and put his hand on her plump arm. "Mary Ann, there is only one of you in the world."

She brightened, and smiled whimsically seeing the love in his eyes for her. "Sure the world can thank the Almighty for sparing it another."

"I beg to differ, it could use a battalion of Mary Anns."

The whitened head lifted, the cheeks turned to scarlet as she marched up the stairs, smiling to herself.

He turned and walked to the window looking out upon the bleak landscape. "A battalion," he smiled – "Dunsany was talking about the fever of war mounting around us—the fever of turmoil in our own land." The sounds of the assassin's boots running down the alleyway at Tunney's aroused his anger further. "I must talk to Matt McGoon down at Donaghmore. They say he is recruiting Irish Volunteers. Now's the time to act on it. The hell with the verses."

Before he had time to go to see McGoon and sign up for the Volunteers, he received a letter from Dunsany asking him to return to Dublin with haste. He never mentioned what the reason was, but Francis knew his friend well enough to know he had something important he wanted to discuss with him.

He made the trip back to Dublin looking at the mirrored image of himself, dark and solitary, in the train compartment window. The clacking of the wheels and the sight of the low ominous clouds swirling outside sent a shiver of deep loneliness for Ellie—gone from him forever.

I'd make my heart a harp to play for you
love songs within the evening of dim day
Were it not dumb with ache and with mildew
of sorrow withered like a flower away.

He stopped suddenly and whispered, "Ellie take me with you, don't leave me here to suffer the years without the sound of your voice—without…" his voice broke, and the sobs hidden so long filled the empty compartment as the broken spectre wept and cursed the darkness of his soul.

## Ourselves Alone

Each year in early spring when the countryside awakened and drew breath, Dunsany held a ball at Adare Manor. Friends from the surrounding villages, and the Abbey Theatre, came to renew friendships with each other and their host for a long weekend of hunting, riding, and story telling. Needless to say the succulent lamb and mutton, and the salmon served fresh and smoked accompanied with wheaten bread and a well stocked wine cellar, made the affair one to be remembered.

The gardens were yielding their first spring pastels and the lawns their deep blue greens. The manor itself seemed cleansed of winter and the uncarpeted floors took on a rosy gleam of polish and light as if relieved of winter's drab and cold.

Dunsany arrived from Dublin on Thursday alone. He had invited many of the Abbey staff, but knew that of that number, perhaps four would attend. Ledwidge had gone to Navan to visit Mary Ann and to plan for the future. Going back home as he referred to Navan, seemed to give him a peace of mind lacking in the brisk pace of Dublin life.

"Ah well," mused Dunsany to himself as he sat in the sedan's backseat looking out over the Derryveagh Mountains, "Visiting Navan will refresh the boy." He smiled, "He probably will have more verses upon his return."

He leaned back against the soft leather and wondered, "Where do our thoughts originate—in the heart, a pump that keeps this frail body alive—or the soul, that unseen often denied source of who we truly are—or perhaps the mind that many sponge-like nautilus whose mysteries are still hidden?" He paused sitting up, "I'm a playwright. I should be able to define the creative act by God!"

The sedan jolted violently, throwing him against the side of the car. "Good God, Charles. Eyes open up there, we can't have a bruised host greeting his guests tomorrow!" Dunsany smiled at the prospect of himself with an arm in a sling and head wrapped in bandages. "Come to think of it, it might make for an interesting story," he laughed. The car turned cautiously down the long avenue of trees, leaving spirals of dust as it made its way towards the house.

The salon, a huge high-ceilinged room to the right of the library, was seldom used during the year. It was the perfect room for great events. Its many windows overlooked the broad acres of gardens and distant mountains surrounding the manor.

Saturday evening the guests gathered in the main salon. Dunsany warmly greeted each of his friends at the door.

The room was filled with small tables and gilt chairs where groups of guests laughed and chatted amicably. Garlands of begonias and similar lay on each table. Golden-rimmed plates and Waterford crystal glittered in the candlelight, and the moving about of servants with platters of smoked salmon and roast lamb added to the overall merriment of the scene. Dunsany, seated at a table near the entrance of the room, was talking animatedly to Sean O'Casey, who in somewhat rumpled evening attire, looked ill at ease and seemed not to be enjoying the evening as much as the others.

"Come now Sean, put away those dark thoughts about the uprising. We hold the mirror up to reflect man, not the savage in these cruel times." O'Casey looked up sadly, "We poets and singers of song, we who hold pens instead of guns," he sighed and went on as the conversation at the surrounding tables became hushed and turned toward the thin bespeckled speaker.

"In 1916, Dunsany, it is. The blood of our youth dries in the streets and behind the hedges. Europe itself girds for battle. Our war has never ceased for centuries. All goes well in Dublin still. The clergy preach and the Salvation Army still trolls out the Customs House Bridge: Glory for me, glory for me; that'll be the glory, glory for me! The pubs are doing their best to satisfy their patrons—the children in the slums still run about naked and hungry; the hospitals and theatres are always full; and the sneering moon looks down and laughs quietly at all of us. Oh life, Oh Man, Today a worm; tomorrow a god; today a god; tomorrow a worm again. Just as you say Dunsany, I try to laugh at the world—no, I do not laugh at the world, but with the world, for a cheerful spirit will serve a man in Heaven or in Hell."

O'Casey shook his head. Dunsany reached out and touched his arm. The others at the table visibly moved by the words just spoken sat solemn and without comment.

"Sean O'Cathasaigh," Dunsany spoke tenderly using the Gaelic pronunciation of the playwright's name. "It is a god you are—and no worm shall ever be a god. It is not the purpose of the Creator for yourself nor any man. Sean friend, come lift your glass to the cause." The guests stood and lifted their glasses. The talking and laughter ended as table after table wondered what was said.

Dunsany then lifted his glass in a toast: "Ladies and gentlemen—Ourselves Alone—Sein Fein." The stillness that followed the toast was interrupted by O'Casey who, breaking into an unfamiliar but genial smile added, "The land, the sea and the air of Ireland, for the people of Ireland!"

The cheers which broke from the throats in that room could be heard throughout the manor. Far down the valley, the shepherd paused and turned his head towards the lighted windows. If he had but known, his cheer too would have pierced the glory of that night.

## The Heart's Sing

Francis, discouraged after several attempts to work out verses on a nationalistic theme, tore his efforts to shreds and fed them to Mary Ann's small parlor fire. The paper caused a nightly surge sending a multitude of sparks up the chimney and out over the grate. "Incendiary indeed," he muttered dejectedly. He sat staring into the flames as if mesmerized. "Not one of them good, it's just not right. The words are heavy. I do not feel the surging of...," here he paused and smiled a smile of patriotic passion.

He sat up suddenly as if he had discovered an important facet of why he had failed. He laughed a bit, then standing, walked over to the mantle and laid his hand on the small vase filled with dry flowers, souvenirs of spring, and then resumed his monologue.

"You're a damn fool, Ledwidge. The song of patriotism is not in you to put down on paper. Ellie sang her Minstrel Boy, it came naturally to her—the broken note, the minstrel's death, and the ghost singing on more boldly than before with harp accompaniment." He knew that Dunsany would understand the cause and it would be his to write. Somewhere within Francis' soul the singleness of purpose in his existence was to bring sweet echoes of the singers gone, he would pour out upon the empty pages of his notebooks his haunting visions of the flight of blackbirds in the marshes of the Lake of Shilee, to walk the glens of Trim and record the pinks and lavenders of their twilight skies. His future was to speak the Gaeltacht to the farmers and tradesmen of Ormagh and interpret the little people to all with the hearts of children. It was quite simple he thought.

"You're letting your cod roe get cold, Francis. You better be eating." Mary Ann, standing in the doorway, brought him back to the present.

"Good heavens, Auntie, there I was thinking of…" "Of everything but your stomach," she shook her head. "Come, I've gone and made your favorite supper and you're off dreaming. Sure the lass that captures your heart surely won't be a cook, I'm thinking."

Francis smiling, followed her through the door into the kitchen. The roe was a bit cold, but Mary Ann's look of triumph was so beautiful to behold that he said, "Auntie, this is perfection!" The dear lady with the rosy cheeks cocked her head to the side and replied, "You've a grand way with words, Francis Ledwidge. Am I to believe they're true?"

Francis looked up into those loving eyes. "I speak from the heart, Auntie, and I do love everything you do and have done for me. This must have been the right moment for me to have spoken to you of it. Cod roe or no, indeed I speak the truth in that."

How many times after he had left to return to Dublin did that lonely old lady sit in her chair, thimble and needle in hand, looking up now and again repeating the lines to herself that he had spoken. Only when the twilight came, and she suddenly aroused herself to light the lamp did she pause. Then putting away her sewing, she sang snatches of songs from the past with a gladdened heart on her way to prepare her solitary meal.

## Dublin

Dublin was in the middle of another uprising. The Irish Loyalists, the Sinn Fein, and the Irish Republican Army were street fighting the Black and Tans. The city was filled with the smoke of British and Irish gunfire.

O'Connell Street was cut off from the bridge with barbed wire. Francis, hearing the fury of the assault, found an alternate route to his flat and kept to his rooms.

At three o'clock, on February third, two days after he had arrived back in Dublin, a young boy knocked at his door. Opening the door,

Francis nodded for the lad to enter. He took the long white envelope extended to him.

"Pour some tea lad, and cut a slice of bread for yourself." Francis moved towards the light by the windowseat and tore open the letter. The familiar crest greeted him. Dunsany must have been in a great hurry for the print was in sweeping cursive writing.

> Have joined the British Army a fortnight ago. Received my commission as Colonel of His Majesty's Sixth Fusiliers. Please meet me at the theatre at seven this evening. Forgive abruptness of this missive. Will be more explicit when I see you.

Francis was shocked. "Joined the British Army! My God, why not? He may be an Irish landowner and a sympathizer of the cause but he's a British subject."

The young messenger cleared his throat. The sound brought Francis to attention. "Oh yes, I'd forgotten you." Reaching into his pocket and taking a crown, he handed it to the slim fellow.

"Thank you sir for the tea and bread," the lad murmured quietly.

"A pleasure," Francis returned brightly, even though his mood was far removed from frivolity. Still holding the letter, he spoke to himself. "God, I haven't slept through these last months to be awakened by a cannon aimed at Ireland—indeed all of Europe." He looked at his watch and noted he had only to wait a few hours to talk with his patron and learn of the events that had culminated in Sunday's decision to join the army.

## World War

Promptly at seven he found his way into the familiar stalls of the Abbey. The afternoon's performance of O'Casey's play had left its mark in discarded playbills and sticky taffy wrappers. Strange how people could eat during such an emotional play and concentrate on their stomachs rather than on the lines spoken. "I'll never understand," commented Francis shaking his head. "Yet they come—tinker, tailor, sailor, banker, roustabout—no matter, they come," and he smiled.

There sitting under a work light on the small stage sat Dunsany reading some papers.

Hearing Francis' approaching footsteps he rose and shading his eyes peered into the theatre. "That you Francis—always the punctual one. Depend on that."

Francis climbed the three short steps to the stage and grasped the extended hand of his patron. "The army is it Sir? It took me by surprise. My mind has not been on worldly matters these past months."

"I know, I know." Dunsany motioned him to sit on a nearby stool. "By the looks of you, your dear Aunt has expanded your frame with a goodly dose of your favorite dishes. You've regained the healthy color you'd lost. " Here his voice lowered and groping for words, he sighed and decided to get to the matter for the meeting. "Let me tell you what has been on my mind and share with you my decision to join the army."

Francis interrupted. "I hear the Germans are waiting to devour the world."

Dunsany looked up and into the troubled eyes of his protege. "There are many who fear the worst for all free men, Francis."

"You know of course, sir that I belong to the Irish Volunteers. My friend Matt McGoon and I have talked recently of our desire to join the army—to call attention to Ireland's plight which has gone for centuries without resolve. I lay my country's cause in the hands of political giants who I feel are the only ones who can release her from serfdom and restore her to the rightful status as a free Ireland without the British heel."

"This World War," Dunsany interrupted, "may be the vehicle to show all countries those who are threatened by tyranny and greed. Much of war lies in the greed of tyrants. All men who fight for the principles of freedom have in the long view improved their individual causes such as your own, lad."

Francis sat staring into the darkened theatre. "If that were true and the future was mine to see, I'd join that army and in serving ultimately serve my very own country," he sighed, and stood, then slowly walked towards Dunsany who looked at him sadly.

"I didn't ask you to join with me. I wanted you to be one of the first to know my decision. It, in no way, was done to enlist your services. No poet has a right to use a rifle. The pen is a powerful weapon. When the refuse of war is past and enemies become allies over the table of commerce and industry, the poet's lines will be read and reread anew. No wars can stop the heartbeats of the poet's lyrics, for indeed, lad, they are immortal."
"Pershing, Napoleon, and Nelson may stand in the city parks but time will chip and erode their granite remains. Centuries will pass and someone will come upon their ruined monuments and wonder who they were or what they accomplished. Mind you Francis, the pen speaks and is never forgotten as long as man can whisper or shout the truths passed from one generation to another. Your Ireland shall endure while you and others like you live and write about her. No gun or bomb can silence it."

Francis, whose heart had been touched by this display of fervor for a country Dunsany really never knew. He turned to his patron and said softly, "True, I shall write my poetry sir, but I shall also carry a gun, perhaps the two will be of some use to both causes, my own and that of Ireland!"

> *All the dead kings came to me at Rosnaree, where I was dreaming.*
> *A few stars glimmered through the morn,*
> *And down the thorn the dews were streaming*

Francis Ledwidge enlisted as a private in the British Army in July of 1914. He joined the ranks of his patron and friend, Lord Dunsany, in the King's Sixth Fusiliers. Before reporting to camp in Belfast, he took a trip back to Navan to see his aunt and settle his affairs at home before embarking on a life far different than he had ever known.

Early August of 1914 had brought no change to the village he had grown to love.

Navan was a quiet and unassuming as ever. Old Quinn was growing more bent but still lively of mind and generous of spirit. Mary Ann herself had grown plumper but she of the full heart and loving soul was all of home for him. They sat in the parlor one evening a few days before Francis' departure watching the sun cast long shadows over the cottage.

"Is there anything I can be doing for you Auntie—anything you want me to attend to?"

She looked at him sadly wondering why he had decided to join the war and why he had joined the British Army—the enemy—no, no the enemy now had become the Germans.

"Everything is attended to, thank you, Francis."

"Strange isn't it Auntie how the Nationalists wear the British uniform with an Irish badge to make our people known to each other in a war with the enemy who means only but to kill both of us with no concern for what has kept us fighting each other—Ireland and England for two centuries?"

Mary Ann shifted her weight in the chair and leaned forward, eager to catch each word of his low voice that almost seemed not to realize he was talking to her, but to himself.

"Poor lad," she thought. "Twenty-five summers on this earth and so much pain—a father not seen nor concerned about him, a love lost to him, a cause not yet won, a world with a gun to his temple, and he, the maker of verses." She cleared her throat, "Do you think you might be visiting Slane, Francis? I hear your Da is not well. Quinn tells me the stepsons have joined the fight—good reason to escape the farm I'd be thinking. They joined up in Ballymena. I'm thinking they've had enough of the soil. Your Da must be almost sixty-five now and seldom come to Navan. Quinn has it that the farm is run down and things are not going well there."

Francis replied, "To think that five miles down the road is the house in which I was born with its window looking out upon the meadows and there in the distance the mountains of Ballynock filled with my childish reveries. It is as real to me this minute that I speak of it as it was then. It is as if at this very minute…" He lit the lamp and blowing out the match threw it into the hearth. Then seating himself again continued quietly, "It is as if in this very moment the past has come before me and not all of the memories are sad or as bitter to me now as I once thought. You know Auntie, the valley and mountains are dear to me in a way that is hard to explain. It was there that all of what I am was nurtured tenderly and with the compassion and understanding as was needed. I was born there."

"The blossom of the hawthorn bush is delicate, almost fragile. It is difficult to pick it and put it into a jar to place on the windowsill and admire—but the thorns themselves present a challenge to one who desires that bloom. Perhaps a finger whose skin is broken to gain the promised beauty needs to hurt—to suffer in order to capture the blossom. Perhaps all that hurt me in that little cottage—that lack of understanding of what I wanted to become—that pain that I endured and the exile I was subject to was needed for me to become what I am now."

Francis was at first surprised at this analysis of the past. He then rose and went over to Mary Ann and lifting her to her feet kissed her cheek. "Now that I'm grown I see that I've become a pathetic scribbler whose verses will soon be forgotten. Da was right. I could have kept my dreams on the farm and today Ledwidge farm would be known throughout the country as the most successful dairy farm in Meath. Mr. Ledwidge and son would have caps tipped to them as they arrived in Navan wearing the best that Dublin drapers could design for two successful gentleman farmers from Slane."

"You've an imagination lad, and that is the truth. If you had decided that if your father had wanted you to be a priest, you'd have it that you'd be the next Pope." Mary Ann laughed and went over to the shelf above the hearth. There, she lifted the sea conch he had given her years before. She motioned to him to join her. Lifting the conch to his ear she whispered, "And what is it you'd be hearing Francis?"

He smiled tenderly and said softly—"The sea, Auntie!" Mary Ann smiled and said to him with tears in those kind eyes, "It will always be the same. That is the sound the conch always sings just as the lonely trees in winter sing of a sadness that we all recognize as their song." Francis said quietly, "It is you who are the poet, Auntie."

The color rose to her pale cheeks. "I'm thinking lad it could be in the blood." He nodded and seeing the grin upon her lovable face added, "Indeed, Mary Ann, and so it is."

Next morning dawned and the sun—iridescent—struck the window and reflected directly on Francis' bed. He had wanted to get an early start to Rosnaree—the wood of the Kings—just off Slane Road. This glorious place was one of his favorite haunts. It lay along the banks of the Boyne River. He dressed quickly, breakfasted lightly, and taking the wicker hamper prepared by his aunt the night before, left the house just as old Quinn was rounding the bend getting an early start on Mary Ann's garden.

"Off on a holiday Francis?" the old fellow inquired.

"Indeed I am Quinn, this is the best time of the day for travel before the sun grows too hot."

"Enjoy the day lad—and go with God!"

Francis thought how many would send you off with this ancient wish and why did it make his trip seem now more important. He looked back over his shoulder and waved to the old gentleman and responded, "And God go with you Quinn."

By noon he had reached the turnoff. The day was growing increasingly warm. He swung over the stile that led close to the Boyen knowing the breeze off her cool water would make the trip more pleasant.

The blackbirds swept past him in groups of two or more spiraling over the water to perch on the high branches of the giant trees lined along the banks. Golden gorse bent in the breeze and the sky above was free of clouds. He unfolded a small cover from the top of the wicker basket and placing it before a broad trunked oak seated himself to watch and listen to the Boyne rushing past him.

*All the dead kings come to me*
*At Rosnaree, where I was dreaming.*

*A few stars glimmered through the morn,*
*And down the thorn the dews were streaming.*

He spoke to the wind and the river at his feet. This is where Cormac saw the glory of Christ as Lightning from the East! In 1690 it was by surprise crossings at Rosnaree ford and Slane that the Williamites turned the Joabolites left flank and made their position in front of Donore untenable. This Battle of the Boyne was the last stand of Gaelic Ireland. From here came the famous lament of one of King James army after 1691:

*At the Boyne River we took our first beating.*
*From the bridge of Slane there was great retreating*
*And then we were tested at Aughrim too*
*Ah, fragrant lovely Ireland—that was goodbye to you*

He looked with sadness at meadow and river. He knew that some hundred years from now, someone would be seated in this very place watching the Boyne as he was now. Someone would look up into the blue dome above and hear the wind rise and fall among the trees which had stood before Cormac so long ago. "Fragrant lovely Ireland—never goodbye to you. Defeat will never be yours dear land of mine." He thought to himself. "I shall be Cormac and Bour. The burial mounds along the river will yield their dead vanquished soldiers and the ancient kings who rest in Newgrange and Knowth will rise and join me. I know who will walk beside me and knowing that I shall not lack courage."

He decided the day before he returned to duty and assignment in Belfast to walk the road to Slane. He had turned over the years in his mind and thinking that once he left Ireland this time he might never return, he decided to see his father. He thought it best not to let Mary Ann know his plans for he might, as he had done before, turn back at the very door!

He walked briskly down the lane to Navan with head bent and shoulders hunched deep in memory. Surely it was fitting for a son who was going to war to say farewell to an ailing father. The day was soft with a light gentle mist sending rainbows between the tall green stalks of grass. Droplets of water pearls clung to the tips of the tree leaves poised to drop soundlessly onto the rich brown earth below. As he rounded the road which led to his boyhood home, he felt a melancholy again envelop him. The road was without vehicle or pedestrian. He could see its curving path winding through the valley. To his right were the Ballynock Mountains standing tall and proud with misty clouds hanging like crowns above the tallest peaks. Looking up Francis stopped and muttered, "Aged yet with no sign of age, like the sea—century upon century the eternal tide—always young. We who pass by grow old and die—you continue each season born anew."

He decided to try his short cut to the back of the farmhouse. It would lessen his trip almost by a half hour. Vaulting over the stone fence, he sprinted through the meadow and climbed a promontory that stretched horizontally along the road but allowed the voyager a broader visage of the serene and majestic scene before him.

The cattle didn't seem to be grazing and the sheepfold was empty as he came upon the hill which looked down upon his birthplace.

The cottage looked smaller than he remembered it. The thatch was in disrepair and the garden overgrown. Could it be his father had worsened? Surely Mary Ann or Quinn would have heard. He started to run, his mouth dry and heart pumping wildly. Damnable pride—foolish pride had kept him from his own flesh and blood. Now death was his own enemy who might soon claim him. He felt he may have come too late and that death might have already taken his father from him.

He raced towards the cottage and reaching the door smoothed his tousled hair and tapped lightly. No sound. Once again he knocked this time, louder. The sound of the knocker broke the silence about him. It was so still the birds had ceased their singing. He tried once more but no sound came from within. His hands wet with anxiety, lifted the latch on the door. It yielded and he stepped into the parlor. It had not changed. His frame filled the small room. The chair, the wooden table, the hearth, and the window looking out upon the lane was the same. The hawthorn bush now almost covered the other window facing the shed. He called, "Da?" He turned quickly to the stairs and climbed them three at a time. He checked his father's room—open—the bed empty. "My God—I'm too late," he moaned.

He walked slowly into each small room now vacant of tenants. It was as if no one had ever lived in this sad place. Little laughter had cheered its walls and soft and lilting voices had left no ghosts. The only sound now was the rustling of the ivy across the parlor window. He decided to return to Navan and tell Mary Ann what had happened. Perhaps the news might not be as bad as he anticipated and perhaps a neighbor had brought Patrick to his farm to care for him. He walked towards the front door slowly retracing his foot prints over those of the child that he had once been, when he looked at the old shelf in the corner of the kitchen, his eyes widened as he turned and walked towards it. There were three books each leaning upon each other. He picked them up. There was the Bible and two titles he knew well—*Songs of the Blackbird*, and *Seascapes*—the poems of Francis Ledwidge. He opened each and saw that they had been read and reread. The peat stains at the edges of the pages revealed their reader was a man who worked close to the soil. "Oh God, don't let me have come too late." A tear streamed down his cheeks and fell upon the open page.

*Above me in their hundred schools*
*The magpies bend their young to rules*
*and like an apron full of jewels*
*the dewy cobweb swings*

## Trim

The village of Trim lies south of Slane and in 1916 was a tranquil and ancient village with farmers as its predominant tenants. The Sisters of St. Brendan O'Maise lived in and tended the old and destitute in a home deeded to them by a deceased gentleman who thought that by this act of charity he would gain enough plenary indulgences to bypass the gates of purgatory and arrive directly at the doorstep of Paradise. It was here that Patrick Ledwidge had come to die. He was left with his fading memories of hard and bitter years of unrewarded toil. Patrick had grown older quickly and was filled with the hopelessness of maintaining the farm. Two days before Francis' return home, the pastor of the church of St. Brendan's had passed Patrick, sitting sadly on a bench outside his cottage staring at some distant scene quite oblivious to the young priest who pulled his trap to a halt and looked at his lost lamb with pity. "Good morning to you Patrick Ledwidge. Dreaming of days past?"

Ledwidge looked up at the priest with hard and bitter eyes and snapped, "Be about your own business. You're wasting your time here."

The priest's jaw dropped and his pale blue eyes took on a glitter as he stiffened. His lean frame and collar tightened so much that his long neck seemed to rise higher with each word he spoke, "Patrick Ledwidge, you're ill and a broken man who no longer can be treated with a kind word. You're to pack up what you will need and come with me to St. Brendan's where the good sisters will tend you with care." Taking a deep breath and surprised at the tone of authority he heard himself assuming, he continued, "I'll not be coming back with my black case without making every effort—my last effort to extend your stay here on earth longer until Christ Himself summons you in spite of your perversity. You'll be coming with me now."

Ledwidge startled by the priest's demeanor, rose to his feet holding on to the windowsill to steady his trembling body. His eyes looked towards the cottage and then to the pasture. "It's time for me to leave this place," he said looking at the priest who now seeing he had won over the pathetic creature lowered his gaze to the man's muddied boots.

"Be you wanting anything from the house before we leave?"

Ledwidge thought a moment and turning sadly to the priest said, "No father, everything I need is here." He pointed one finger to his head. The priest latched the door and lead Patrick slowly to his trap. Once the priest had Patrick in the seat, he placed a blanket about the man's knees. Then he sprang up beside his rescued lamb and signalled the pony with the rein and urged him in the direction of St. Brendan's. If the priest had postponed his visit to Ledwidge by one day, Francis would have seen his father and a reunion might have changed the lives of both men.

Francis stood in the fading light beside the doorstep his father had so recently vacated and looking down the lane he was unable to see the priest's trap marks still visible in the dirt. If only some divine intervention had moved him towards that lane, but then how could mere mortals know who was in that trap and all that had transpired so short a time ago at this very door? Turning into the house once again, he went to the shelf and took the thin volume of his poetry into his hands. He touched the smudges on the pages gently. Then, he returned the book as he had found it and traveled back to Navan on the same route as he had come.

As he came to the stone fence that led to the Navan road he turned once more to look down the valley towards the little cottage. The sky had turned silver and in the fading afternoon he saw the Ballynock Mountains rising above the valley. From far down the pasture the song of the blackbird shattered the stillness with its sweetness

*And wondrous, impudently sweet,*
*The blackbird sings*
*Half of him passion, half conceit*

Francis knew that he never would see the place again. He saw the empty chairs, the cold hearth, and the vacant rooms. In his heart he heard the lost voices of his father and his schoolmaster, Mr. Madden. The blackbird had sung his farewell.

Mary Ann sat sewing by the hearth and raised her head quickly to meet his glance. "You've been gone all day. I've kept some stew warming. Best you have a bit to eat lad. I'll go to see the priest and check on Patrick's whereabouts in the morning." He put out his arm. "Wait. It is for me to do that Aunt. I've made up my mind. I must finish what I set out to do today. I only hope I'm not too late." He put his arm around her shoulders which trembled under his hand.

She thought," Please God, don't let it be too late for them to come face to face—to bury the hurt before the burden becomes too great to carry longer. I'll go with you" she said softly.

"It's best I go alone dear auntie." His manner was calmer now that the words were spoken. He smiled at the plump figure looking at him so sadly.

"Mary Ann, you're all the family I've had these many years. If I leave this place, as I must, to return to my regiment in the morning, I must see him and perhaps we can part with more kindness between us than we did in the past."

She rushed forward and clasped him and her sobs interspersed with her words. "I pray God the both of you can find forgiveness for all the years of pride between you."

He stiffened at the words. "Pride, damnable pride on both sides. There it is said at last," he spoke fiercely. "Hurt is there too—perhaps mixed with vindictiveness. Who knows how the mind finds reasons to widen the chasm of anger for things best forgotten or forgiven. I've spent these many years nurturing the pride, the hurt, even the anger against my own father while placing no guilt upon myself." He walked to the window and looked out into the darkness. "I've made my own night starless against him—shut him out of my days." He crossed to the stairs. "I can't eat auntie. I'll be up early to visit the priest in the morning. Pray to God Mary Ann, that I may see my father's face and place my hand in his before any more time passes."

He was up and closed the cottage door softly early next morning. Mary Ann padded quietly from her room to the window that looked out upon the lane. She saw his figure moving swiftly onto the dirt road towards the village. "Be merciful, be merciful" she whispered.

Pastor O'Connell answered the bell himself. The ancient table lamp filled the hall with a dull glow in the early morning light. The priest stared at Francis in surprise. "Come in," he motioned to the parlor. "May I be of some service to you?"

He sat in the overstuffed chair and spoke quickly for the tightness in his throat closed over his words so that his voice was constricted. "It's about my father, Patrick Ledwidge." "Of course," thought the pastor. "He's the very replica of my parishioner from Slane." "I'm leaving for Belfast with my regiment on the early train and I have hopes that you may know about my father" and his voice broke. The priest knew little of the Ledwidge clan, for he was only two years in the village. He waited quietly for Francis to grain his composure.

"I've been home to the cottage, Pastor and he was gone. We've not seen each other or corresponded for fourteen years." The ticking of the mantelpiece clock filled the long silence. The priest rose and moved to the visibly tormented soul slumped in the chair, despair wrapped as a cloak about him. Francis slowly lifted his head, and looked into the face of the priest and saw he indeed was too late. The sobs that rose from the depth of his soul were wracking and pitiful.

"Oh God," thought the priest, "how we torment ourselves in this life with words unspoken and pain unrelieved by compassion and forgiveness. What sadness speaks now from this soul and what can I say to ease the hurt and futileness this young man now endures."

The glow from the lamp barely touched the boots of Francis. He sat in a darkness deeper than night and felt a despair that would stay with him for as long as he lived.

Francis returned to Navan and told Mary Ann of his father's passing. They wept together each shedding the tears of mourners who had been already mourning for the past fourteen years and for the reunion between father and son that was never to be.

Mary Ann would visit the graveyard at Trim where Patrick was buried by his own request.

The cottage and land in Slane was willed to Francis alone. He had seen to it that the Sisters of St. Bridget would inherit his share. He had abandoned his birthplace in life and had no claim to it now.

Mary Ann stood in the chill of his departure morning holding a small parcel which she handed to Francis as he boarded the train to Belfast.

A cold mist from the Irish Sea hung in shrouds over the station platform on that November morning of 1916. The stationmaster blew his whistle three short pipes signalling the engineer to begin the journey. Mary Ann, her eyes red and swollen, threw her arms around the son she never had and whispered, "God go with you my Francis." He placing the parcel into his army trenchcoat held the sobbing mother he had never known for a minute then kissed her forehead and said, "Goodbye Auntie, I love you. I will write you soon and often."

The train moved forward into the dimness of the morning with its wheels churning forward shooting sparks into the misty air.

Looking back Francis saw the familiar figure—her arm outstretched in farewell. He put his head back against the seat and looked out the train window seeing his face reflected in the glass and moving behind that face the limestone road that flashed pictures of his beloved countryside before him. The greens, the shades of brown, the whites and yellows, the valleys and the hills and lakes. All too soon the sun lightened the sky and his face had disappeared from the window and left only the lanes and farms making indelible impressions upon his mind and heart.

*This is a song a robin sang*
*This morning on a broken tree*
*It was about the little fields*
*that call across the world to me*

## Belfast

Belfast in 1916 was a maelstrom of activity. The British army had its debarkation area stationed near the Irish Sea. Shopkeepers had full cash registers thanks to the overpopulation of the military.

Innkeepers were never without smiles as their rooms were filled with wives and families of departing patriots eager to stay with their men and sons until the final hour came.

The farmers produce and cattle were at a high premium and in great demand. Belfast was enjoying a prosperity never to be experienced again. Soldiers of the Irish claim to Home Rule mingled with the true Anglican without recognition as the uniform of both were the same.

When Francis reported to the barracks of his Majesty's Sixth Fusiliers he was exhausted from the past day's events and without concern for what would lie ahead for him. He had written Dunsany of the events of the past week knowing he would not be in Belfast himself for yet a fortnight.

The soldier seated at the desk motioned him to a chair. Francis gave him his name and the information that he knew was needed to the efficient and emotionless fellow who having found his papers looked up at the disheveled Irishman before him.

"Dunsany's pet, Damn these so called poets and playwrights. What the hell are they soldiering for—the poor devil can barely put two words together—seems distraught and probably suffering from premature shell shock already!"

"Yes, here we are Ledwidge." Holding the paper in front of him the sergeant read to the listless and apathetic figure forlornly huddled in the chair. "You've a week's furlough extension. Bastard," thought the professional solder. "Grab yourself an officer like Dunsany in the Sixth Fusilier's who is a patron to writers and you find yourself among the privileged!"

Francis raised his head slowly noting the distaste clearly written on the sergeant's face. The sergeant put the folder into a wire rack on his desk and with a brisk "Dismissed" turned his attention to a file wherein he became totally occupied.

Francis sighed, saluted the back of the sergeant's head, and walked out into the cold afternoon. "One week's extension," he thought as he walked along the thoroughfare where several trams stood waiting for soldiers such as himself who still could go to town before receiving military orders that would announce their future.

The sight of the tram brought to mind the memory which lay always close to his mind—Ellie Vaughey—he saw again the tram coming closer and closer to him as he waited for her near Tunney's. He could see her waving to him as she stepped down to greet him and the sound of gunfire followed by boots running down the alley.

"Ellie," he murmured remembering those eyes startled and questioning looking at him. He could feel the softness of her lips as he held her to him. "All that I had is lost to me," he moaned aloud.

"A year ago! it seems but yesterday! yesterday ! a hundred years ! all one!"

## The Inn of the Three Clocks

The Inn of the Three Clocks stood at the top of Carrich Street in the southwest section of Belfast. An old and hospitable place with few military the tram driver had said when Francis boarded Number 12 at the barracks gate. "Yes, lad," said the conductor whose white hair and genial demeanor betrayed a dedicated public servant. "It's a decent place. Those who like the city life and its pleasures draw a wide circle around the Three Clocks." Francis settled back into the back of the tram which was filling up with laughing, jostling soldiers eager to start the furlough that they knew would be their last before embarkation.

As the tram wound its way up and down the street of Belfast, Francis remembered the parcel Mary Ann had pressed upon him back at the Navan station and reached down into the pocket of his coat and laid it on his knees.

The hijinks of the soldiers grew louder as he sat solitary and forlorn holding the parcel and wondering what it might be—a woolen scarf or gloves for the cold? He smiled faintly thinking of the last member of his Family whom he could love and who cared for him in return. The tram lurched to a stop. Francis grasped the parcel as the conductor said, "Three Clocks it is, lad." Thanking the conductor for his help, he alighted and crossed the cobblestone street as a light rain began to fall. The street lamps were just being lighted and the carefully tended houses seem to huddle closer to each other as darkness fell. The Inn of the Three Clocks looked friendly indeed.

He signed the register and climbed the steep stairs to the second floor, bending his head so as not to bump it against the low ceiling. He finally reached the upper hallway.

The doors were all painted brown with a brass number on each door. He looked at his key dangling from a square piece of wood—number 212—his was the last door in the hallway. He turned the key and went in. He lit the gas lamp on the wall near a large dresser and looked at himself in the mirror. A gaunt and unshaven creature holding a key and a parcel returned his stare. Throwing his trenchcoat over the single chair in the room he walked towards the brass bed and slipped the cord from the wrapping of the parcel and looked at its contents. "My books from the cottage in Slane! Mary Ann must have sent Quinn down there during the night when I'd fallen asleep in the chair so as not to miss the train. Could she have gone herself? I wouldn't put it past her!"

There they were, the very books he had found on the old shelf with the imprint of fingers of the dead Patrick lying on some of the pages as bookmarks. He stood holding the books carefully in his hands and looked out into the empty street. The rain had become heavy now and blew in gusts against the windowpanes.

*He will not come, and still I wait*
*He whistles at another gate*
*Where angels listen, Ah, I know*
*he will not come, yet if I go*
*How shall I know he did not pass*

Francis looked down a the worn copy and wept.

## Ian McNabb of Larne

Francis spent the next two days walking the streets of Belfast. He made no friends nor sought any. The pubs were full of the frantic antics of those who felt their life's clock ticking too swiftly. He did however enjoy the crisp November air and the landscape near the Irish Sea. The white thatched cottages bordering the sea were alive with the bantering of the fishermen preparing their boats for the day.

This fishing village was the largest on the coastline and boasted a small community of seamen and their families. They were a hardy group of men with faces burned by the sun and eyes as blue as the sea itself. Their cottages were well cared for and inviting to behold.

"Morning to you soldier lad," a stock seaman of undeterminable age greeted him as he hauled a bucket of snail bait onto the hull with his davit.

"A fair morning it is," replied Francis.

"Be you from Belfast and the camp?," inquired the man.

"Belfast it is, but not for long as I'll be off to Belgium I expect very soon."

"Ah Belgium, a sweet land it is. Can you come aboard and join me for the day; that is if you've got the time? I'd be honored to have you." The smile with the direct invitation warmed Francis and he replied, "Sure I've always wanted to do that sir. This is the first chance I've had, or rather the first invitation extended to me by a true seaman." The blue eyes and round face seemed delighted.

"Ian McNabb—that's my name," and the seaman clasped Francis' hands warmly. Returning the handshake, "I'm Francis Ledwidge and that glad to meet you Mr. McNabb." The oars were placed carefully into the oarlocks and the Nellie O, McNabb's pride and joy, put out into the breaking waves with Francis rowing her solid timbers out past the breakers to the Irish Sea herself. Francis felt as all men of the sea must—the joy of leaving the land behind and bracing to meet the water and sky first hand.

"Nothing like it lad. There isn't a morning that goes by, indeed even a day, when the wind is wild and the sea's choppy that I don't feel the wonder of it all." McNabb took over the oars and soon the village of Larne grew smaller and the seacliffs were the only landmarks where the two had stood together but a short time ago.

Ian McNabb in the course of the next hours, recalled his life in short staccato sentences. The son of a seaman—a native of Larne—a widower with no McNabb's to carry on the sea tradition. But no matter, McNabb had been a happy man and the fates had treated him not too harshly. Francis listened attentively and marveled at the simplicity and completeness of the man.

"Enough of myself," laughed the seaman. "And what of you, Francis?"

"We make a good pair, Ian. for I am a farmer."

"Ah," Ian continued, "the meeting of the land and the sea." Here McNabb reached under the tarpaulin behind him, pulled a basket covered with a checkered napkin, and handed Francis a sandwich carefully wrapped. "I hope you like porksteak, lad."

"One of my favorites," Francis's appetite had been whetted by the sea air and he munched away happily. The two acquaintances sat in the warm noon sun, the boat anchored and heaving gently in the quiet swells of the turning tide. Indeed the wonder of it all!

That evening as McNabb and Francis walked slowly towards the bus that would take Ledwidge back to Belfast the sky was azure and cold, and day hung its light between dusk and the darkness.

"It's been a time I'll long remember," McNabb spoke quietly.

"Will you be embarking soon lad or is it to be a long training period?"

"That, Ian, is in the hands of others than myself. It's up to the commandant, my friend, Edward Dunsany."

"A good man!" Ian turned his steady gaze to Francis's face.

"A very good man indeed." He was about to tell this stranger more when he stopped and for the first time realized he was now a soldier and the role must be lived. The former farmer and writer of pastoral verses was set aside now. He turned to the warm and friendly McNabb and shook his hand.

"A special day it has been Ian and I thank you for it."

"Will you send me a postcard or some news of yourself, lad? Just put McNabb, Larne; it'll get to me proper," returned his new friend.

The approaching bus wheezed and halted. The two shook hands. Francis stepped aboard and smiled. He watched the figure of McNabb standing alone until the bus turned a bend and made its way towards Belfast. Ian McNabb, seaman and Francis Ledwidge, soldier. Strangers—now friends!

## Dunsany

Edward Drax Dunsany was a soldier of discipline and charisma. One would have to have researched his life to guess he was a witty writer of satire and one whose play, *Glittering Gates*, had been presented at the Abbey and directed by Yeats himself. He had a chameleon personality that adapted him to his environment. The men in his company were of two types—one the career soldier and the other the boot soldier who in this particular time in history had been conscripted or had volunteered—the latter out of true patriotism, the other in flight from desperate poverty. Dunsany was respected for his talents as a soldier and his ability to command and lead men. Meeting him two weeks into training seemed like meeting a stranger.

Francis stood at attention. The tired looking aide announced him to Dunsany.

Dunsany moved from behind his desk and placed his hands on Francis' shoulders. "You've grown taller and somehow your color has improved."

"No longer the pale poet," he laughed.

Dunsany stepped back and before he could say another word Francis told him about the death of his father, and his discovery of his books. Dunsany smiled sadly.

"Too late, always too late. It's as if fate marks us for these reunions and then for some reason it can never be."

"No, I don't think it was to be that I would see and talk with him, sir. I think it best it happened as it did. When do you expect us to embark?" The questions seemed incongruous in one sense—moving so quickly from past to the present.

*Death is as interesting to me as life*
*I am always homesick.*
*I hear the roads calling, and the hills and the rivers*
*wondering where I am.*

## Ypres 1917

The Belgium summer of 1917 was hot and humid. The countryside of Ypres in the southwest farm country was empty of tenants. The hedges alone were bursting with blooms. All else was war's desolation as the column of British and French troops moved down a two cart lane leading to an old farmhouse battered by German shells. A voice shouted, "Take shelter in the fields and dig yourselves in men. Sergeant, take your platoons and see each trench is high enough for each man to stand in." The voices of the soldiers mingled with the commands of their superiors. Soon the clump-clump of shovels striking the earth punctuated the silence of the meadows around the farmhouse and barn. "The Krauts are ahead of us, eh Francis," puffed Clement Timmons, a muscular man who had been a lorry driver in London.

"Well, If having the high ground, with plenty of wire around you and of course being in advance of us to set up your position, qualifies you for making that observation," smiled Francis, "then you are speaking the truth." Clement smiled broadly and straightened up to stretch his weary muscles and wipe the perspiration from his thick neck.

"Ledwidge my friend, we have been chasing these Kaiser lads now for ten miles and they can't say we give up easy." As Clem was speaking, the sun slid with relief toward the horizon, hovered briefly to look upon the scene of war, and then retired to allow the moon to take its turn over the part of the world where few would care to observe the brutality of men and nations.

Ledwidge padded the wet earth from the back of his shovel and propped it to the side of the trench, and surveyed the helmet tops and the trenches that surrounded him. All these weeks we spent training only to kill and yet to survive he thought. The drills, the maps, the voices of Captains and Sergeants barking orders and directions filled his brain.

Dunsany had stayed at the command post a mile behind the frontal force to reconnoiter and plot the newest foray to rout the Germans at Ypres. They were now in their third battle and still the German forces prevailed.

A light tapping sound came from the rear trench as the moon lit up the field. Ledwidge smiled. Denny, the resident shoe repairman, was setting up his cobbler shop for business. His wooden sign, with the charcoaled words "shoe repair" announced to all the men that boots could be repaired to usability and perhaps a strip of leather salvaged from God knows where could replace a worn out sole and ease the march of these tired feet forward to strike once more at the Germans. Francis marveled at the men around him in all sizes and dimensions from farms, villages, and cities whose trade in spite of the situation seemed to rise above the fact that there was a war yet they served the needs of one another. Matt Findley, a tailor in peace time was over to the right near the stonewall. His little scrap of lumber read sewing repairs! Where they found the materials was something no one really thought too much about but it was always there! Now if their luck held out business would continue as usual.

## War

Dunsany's two-seater cycle broke the silence of the early morning with its backfiring and wove zigzagging towards the farmhouse. He had aged more in these months of the skirmish than he had realized, as did the British Exploration Forces. In all these months they had not advanced ten miles. Their losses had been higher than one hundred and thirty thousand and the overall view was disheartening. The Germans had selected the high ground and had barbwired communication lines around themselves. They also had concrete pillboxes. The BEF were still learning the technique of trench warfare! Talk about how to bring the Germans to their knees back in Belfast was totally lacking in the reality they now faced.

Dunsany, with boots gleaming and baton clutched to his side, strode to the rear of the barn where a captain and his sergeant were huddled over a water trough covered with a large wooden plank which served as a map table planning the day's strategy.

"Good morning Payne," Dunsany spoke solemnly. Captain Payne, a Sandhurst and Christ College graduate, looked up.

"Good morning sir." Dunsany liked Payne. He was straightforward, valiant, and reliable.

"Can't we get some artillery help that could break up those concrete boxes and give us a look at the enemy sir?"

Dunsany smiled, "Getting tired of just bullets—want to see the Germans face to face eh Captain?"

Payne interrupted, "I think if we could see the buggers we'd soon know he was flesh and blood. sir."

"I quite agree," Dunsany replied spiritedly. The group huddled over the map once again and went over the terrain with Dunsany pointing out their goals with his baton. An orderly cleared his throat as the soldiers backed away from the table and announced

"Coffee sir?" No one spoke but each to a man reached for their tins and thin wisps of steam pencilled their way up in the damp July morning.

The rank and file soldiers climbed from their night's hostel, moved toward the lane on command, then fell into a file side by side in close order. They shifted their guns and tightened the leather straps under their chins. "Just another morning," Francis thought, and another day—one after another both bleak an desolate. His contingent had never as yet seen battle; but this morning they all realized this was the day they would at last meet up with the Germans.

They passed a group of British soldiers with vacant eyes and exhausted bodies returning from the front line. The sound of their boots lifting the earth in puffs of white dust was like a clock thumping out the seconds and minutes. The explosions of shells in the higher elevations honing towards them rang in their ears. "Maybe today," muttered Francis.

A linnet sang in an alder tree—its voice sweet and haunting—Francis missed a step. He turned and then bumped into Clement who doggedly trudged forward murmuring "Now what the hell is that bird singing for. He ought to have flown away long ago." Francis picked up the thought and let his memory take hold of him. "Yes, it sounded like the linnet who sang that day he visited the Meeting of the Waters near Rosnaree. It couldn't be the same one. Could birds fly great distances he wondered!"

"Ledwidge day dreaming is it," asked Clem. The other men caught up in their own thoughts seemed not to hear. "It's a bad habit I'm trying to rid myself of."

"Not at all laddie. Anything that takes one's mind off this business should be indulged." The sun grew hotter as the day progressed. At noon they could see the dark puffs of shell explosions ahead. The earth shook under their feet. A whistle blew and they moved into an apple orchard that lined both sides of the dirt road. The food lorries moved up and there in the sultry sun and bombardment a mile forward, they dined with their tins for the midday meal, perhaps their last.

The orchard spread as far as the eye could see. One of the two white-washed barns sat next to a stream to their left. Only the chimneys remained. Francis moved away from his platoon and walked down to a grove of trees hardly tasting the rations from his tin. He lay down under a huge elm and gazed at the pale blue sky. The periodic thumps of shrapnel seemed like heartbeats and were the only reminder of where he was. A whistle blew and broke his reveries. Once again he moved towards his contingent who were packing their tins in their pouches ready to move forward onto the road.

The rain came suddenly. Streaks of heat lightning had jettisoned across the late afternoon sky. Now sheets of rain whipped by the wind slashed across the men pulling them forward and in its wake the piping of sergeants' commands tore through the fury of the elements. Thunder at times silenced the artillery.

"Take shelter men. Dig in deep. They don't stop the war at sunset you know." The words echoed and reechoed across the fields. Out came the pointed metallic short shovels and once more the putty-like earth was invited to shelter fragile man. Again the bombardment challenged the thunder.

"Damn," muttered Ledwidge. "Mud and more mud," complained Clement whizzing and puffing to thirty feet from Francis swearing with every shovel of dirt he lifted.

"Can I be dropping you off at the Dorchester, Sir Francis, and then be picking you up to go to the Savoy for kidneys and trifle?" Clem never finished his invitation as Francis let fly his shovel, which hitting Clem's knee, laid him flat on his face savoring the bitter mud that now was the first course of the evening's proclivities!

The night was alive with lightning, thunder and the screeching of shells. The men stood in the dripping trenches. The heat and humidity prevailed despite the wind. No man's land, that part of the soggy earth between trenches thirty to eighty feet forward and rear, was a crater of water. The men were soaked to the skin and the water whipped by the wind covered and washed their faces with liquid earth. The rain fell like machine gun pellets on their helmets and reminded them they were to be grateful the rain was not as lethal as a bullet.

Sometime around dawn, the rain, the fury of lightning, and the whining of shells, ended. A silence fell over the encampment.

"Clem?" Francis whispered to his friend as he moved himself out of the water logged trench to a more solid piece of ground. The men around him had begun coming out of their trenches and were cursing the weather that had engulfed them these past watery hours. Francis crawled toward Clement's trench. He looked down. "My God," he moaned. Clem face down in the trench, had drowned! The rain had filled up during the night, and Clement bone tired, had slept not realizing he had dug so deeply. He became the first of the contingent to die. The men were horrified. This they never expected to drown on a field of battle! Francis pulled the stiffened form out of his trench and knelt in shock beside him.

"Make way here," shouted the sergeant pushing the men aside who now silently stood looking upon the first casualty of their personal war.

"Let this be a lesson to you men. This is the result of digging too deeply," the sergeant growled.

"That is what you told us to do sir. To protect us best from the enemy's fire. You never did mention the rain being another adversary." The men mumbled agreement. Francis and the sergeant lifted Clement to a waiting lorry where attendant's took charge. The sergeant took Clem's tags and placed them into his knapsack—noted his name and serial number into a small folder and then nodded to the attendants who closed the lorry's doors, started the engine, and drove back down the road. Francis followed the truck, his feet shuffling and his head, down upon his chest.

"Ledwidge," the sergeant barked. "Report back to your platoon. We're moving up now—nothing can be done here. Bad luck, lad." Francis stiffened and lifted his head and turned towards the group whose eyes stared straight ahead but whose faces reflected none of the sadness that Francis' face held. He turned one last time to gaze at the disappearing lorry. He whispered aloud, "pray for those of us left."

The earth shook with explosions. The German pillboxes spat their bullets incessantly. The strategy was to wait until the British artillery unit moved forward and gained position on a small hill to the left of the meadow to train their grey muzzles towards the enemy on the hill above.

Wire surrounded each German pillbox and the bodies of the dead British soldiers spread like carrion across section after section of wire like grotesque dolls with their arms and legs in an agonized death dance. Captain Payne rolled out the makeshift map on the back of the Red Cross truck's floor and with the Sergeants of the forward platoons studied the situation without emotion.

"Unless we get the barrage our boys promised as backup, we've got to withdraw to the village there at Messines." He pointed his forefinger to a square on the wrinkled map. The sergeants nodded. "This is the third time we've tried to roust these bastards sir. These Bosch have tough hides." Payne remained stoically studying the map, his jaw working on some plan other than retreat.

"Things go on as usual," someone piped. "Do you expect high tea regular each day?" spoke out a redfaced sergeant. "We're in a war now you know."

Captain Payne cleared his throat. "Save that lads, I want you to fall back at 20 hours. We should have darkness when we go back to Messines. Our scout has reported the village secure. We'll be out of reach of their guns. Our artillery boys can clean up those filthy concrete boxes. Then we can regroup and send those bastards to bloody hell." The sergeants and platoon leaders nodded assent. A young lieutenant jumped to the ground from a lorry and walked briskly back to the platoon. "Why in God's name hadn't they done that to begin with." Too late to apologize to the poor blokes on the wire.

Ledwidge had for some time been thinking of Slane when Clement drowned. "Was it only two days before?" He had suddenly awakened to the reality of where he was. This was his first experience in battle. He hadn't even fired his rifle. He had for the past month been walking and shoveling himself into the earth like an animal. The bleakness of the country now and the blackened trees, the whine of shells, and his brief encounter with death but a foxhole away, tore the veil his mind had dropped heretofore on grim reality. Now, as his platoon marched back down the dirt road, his thoughts turned back to Mary Ann. He was only twenty seven years old. His feet moved right left right left. "Back to Messines" the platoon lead had said. Only the sound of "scuff scuff" and the rattle of their shovels hitting their meal tins on their belts was heard. The guns were silent. The Germans were human too and besides no use to waste ammunition on those retreating.

"Pick em up," Sergeant McCoy peppered them with his commands. He wondered what McCoy did before all this. Probably serviced the trains at Victoria Station or called the Rugby scores at his public school. Francis smiled. "Was it still possible!"

"Can you share that smile with me lad?" The sergeant was next to Ledwidge matching him step for step. Francis looked straight ahead and answered, "You've a voice sir that commands respect." The sergeant thought a minute and looked again at Francis' now serious face.

"You're not putting me on lad?"

"No sir."

"Well, now I take that as a compliment. I do thank you!" The sergeant was leading his squad in retreat seemed, if only to himself, to be leading them to victory! "Who would think," thought Francis, "that a small gesture of kindness as he had made had been taken so seriously by the poor devil. God help us, God help us all."

*The hills are crying from the fields to me*
*And calling me with music from a choir*
*of waters in their woods where I can see*
*the bloom unfolded on the whein like fire.*
*And, as the evening moon climbs ever higher*
*and beats away the shadows from the slope.*
*They cry to me like things devoid of hope.*

## The Shouts of Warriors

Dunsany stood by the wireless at camp headquarters which was a farming village ten kilometers east of Messines. The tap—tap of the wire spoke the news. Fourteen days of heavy rain had bogged down guns and transportation. French armies had suffered severe casualties at Arras east of the Ypres line causing mutiny among the troops. Because of the failure of their attack and casualties, Nievelle, the French Commander, was replaced by General Henri Petain. The British at this time had suffered four hundred thousand casualties which still did not result in penetrating the German lines!

Dunsany moved to the doorless farmhouse and looked out at the dead village—a wagon lying overturned, the gate to a pasture intact—a hay rack on its side—the earth muddy and desolate. "I hope to God the Americans can turn things around. They're in it now." He took a cigarette from the case in his pocket and inhaled deeply. "I wonder how Ledwidge is making out—imagine a man such as he facing a gun or using one for that matter." He spoke to himself as the others were still huddled as usual around the wireless listening to the news. The United States declared war on Germany on 3 April 1917.

Captain Payne and his men arrived at Messines. A winery was now headquarters for Payne's platoon. He stood near a shelled out wall in the winery and looked over to the horizon. "It's hard to realize that we stand on French soil and we are British, and that down the road, eight miles North, the Germans are in concrete pillboxes and firing down on land that belongs to no one—in truth!" Payne stepped back into the room and paced back and forth speaking as if to himself.

"If only someone could end the fighting and plotting. Those men would have it in their power to end this destruction and restore these villages and hundreds like them to the peace they have a right to possess."

"Excuse me sir," Sergeant McCoy interrupted. "How many would be needed and who would agree as to whom they would be these men of power?"

Payne stopped his monologue at this intrusion. "Quite right, sergeant. There would be a bloody fight to decide that and a lifetime deciding who would have the spoils of war. The knights of old simplified it by the tournament—the one down is the vanquished—the other, the victor."

"We're not in the Middle Ages sir," piped up someone.

"I rather wish we might have been," sighed Payne, shaking his head and wishing now he hadn't begun his futile mental meandering concerning the war. "Sergeant," Payne spoke briskly, "Give the men a bit of reprieve before we start up again—extra rations. You know what to do. Let them have a little time to put their shovels to rest before we start back out again."

"I'll take care of it, sir", snapped the sergeant and moved toward his squad some of whom were leaning against the shed and the rest scattered across in front of the winery. "High tea it is lads." The platoon looked at each other suspiciously each thinking the same thought. "Now where in the hell did the old sergeant major dear find the wine, we didn't! Could it be the building he just came out of had hidden chambers below ground that they had not discovered!"

Francis had found a small spot next to an old mill about four hundred yards from the ruined farmhouse. Now that Captain Payne had issued orders to give the troops a boost in morale, he had commandeered this quiet place to draw himself together in mind and in spirit.

"My God, these past weeks have been a limbo," he murmured to himself. "I haven't felt anything except poor Clem's tragedy." He pulled off his shoes and unwrapped the soiled puttees and tossed his socks into the stream and placed a large stone on top of the socks to keep them from moving downstream. Then placing his calloused feet into the cool water, he fell back onto the soft grass. Staring at the sky, and the grass of Ballymore Valley, he closed his eyes and thought. "Same sky, God, and there in Ballymore, no doubt the same. I long to get up and walk down the road to the village below Messines and change into a peasant's clothes, and join the ever moving crowds of refugees that wander toward the coast." He wondered if he would ever see the sea again.

"Ledwidge," Payne stood casting a shadow over him and he jumped to his feet. "Day dreaming there be you?" He looked down at his bare feet. Payne laughed. "Put your socks on man; you've got a visitor. We've got the cream here today Private. Company Commander Dunsany, his adjutant, and Sir Douglas Haig, Director of British Forces. This day shall go down in history. I can tell my grandchildren I shook hands with those who took us to victory."

"You say Commander Dunsany is here!" Francis never thought he'd see him again.

He struggled into his socks cursing his foolishness in leaving them in the water. He pulled his boots on, wound the puttees around his legs, then followed Captain Payne towards the winery in front of which was the Company Commander's staff car.

Dunsany stepped out of the door and grasped his outstretched hand warmly. Francis forgetting to salute, smiled at his friend then he quickly stood back and saluted realizing his mistake.

"I was thinking I'd not see you again sir with all that's happening."

Dunsany searched the familiar face. "Tougher" he thought. "Perhaps the army can change the appearance of a man quickly but can it change the man into a machine for death and remove all that he was or is?"

"Sir?"

Dunsany bit his lip. "The news may be that we march to Ypres in a day or a week at most. I would imagine not much longer than that. No orders yet. Just guessing."

"Sit down, sit down. I've lots on my mind now and I'm afraid I'm not making too much sense to you. I wish I could be more definitive but I can't."

"Of course sir. I understand."

Dunsany lifted his hand to interrupt but Francis spoke on emptying the thoughts that filled his mind.

"Sir, I joined this unit because of my respect for you. If I stayed in my village with the Volunteers I could not raise my voice against this bigger war."

Dunsany shook his head, "God is kind, and events shape strange patterns. Some good comes from these I believe and this meeting proves me right." Here Dunsany turned to the other officers present and introduced Francis to each in turn.

"Sir Douglas," Dunsany paused in front of his Commander in Chief. "Sir Douglas, this is my friend and literary colleague, Ledwidge."

Sir Douglas Haig, his handsome face and six foot two frame seemed perfectly cast as a leader of men, shook Francis' hand enthusiastically. "The world will have need of poetry such as yours when this ordeal is finished, my boy. Edward here has often spoken of your talents. I too before all this," his head nodded to the scene about them, "often went to the Abbey and thought highly of your mentors." Dunsany smiled appreciatively. "Your poetry was just about to become more known before the Kaiser put his foot into history," Sir Douglas continued.

Francis, finding himself overwhelmed by this attention, cleared his throat.

"I shall never know if anyone a year from now ever will have heard of Francis Ledwidge except of course for my aunt Mary Ann and Lord Dunsany."

"Take nothing for granted young man. If the people who you have mentioned remember you, that's prize enough. They seem to come from different stations in life and if they think the best of you, who could ask for more?"

With these remarks Haig turned back into the room and motioned to the officers present to get on with the business of the day designing a plan of attack that would break the German defenses.

Francis walked with Dunsany as far as the staff car.

"Have you heard from your aunt, Francis?"

"Regular as the mail. It is the one thing I wait daily for. As soon as I open her letters, she's with me. It's like we were sitting in the parlor, sipping tea, and hearing the news of the village and neighbors."

Dunsany spoke quickly. "You know of course the Yanks are in it now and with God's help we'll end this hell and go back to living."

"That day, I pray can't come too soon."

Dunsany, his eyes saddened replied, "It will come, God knows that it will." Then shaking Francis' hand, he turned and rejoined the group inside.

Francis turned to see the sergeant and some of the men watching him.

"Manage to get us relief lad?" smiled the sergeant. "Is it a day or a fortnight now that we can go back home?"

Francis spoke nervously, "If I had my way Sergeant, we would be taking the first step toward home at this moment!" The group outside the winery looked up as a shout of approval broke the silence in the yard outside. Moving to the windows Dunsany and the other men smiled to see Francis, high up on the shoulders of his buddies, being carried ceremoniously down the road with the ever present Sergeant McCoy bringing up the rear laughing as the squad tossed Francis's cap into the air and catching it without dropping it once!

"Now what was that about?" asked Sir Douglas of Dunsany.

"Francis probably declared an Armistice, sir."

Sir Douglas smiled. "I hope the Germans hear about it."

*From hill to hill, from land to land*
*Her lovely hand is beckoning for us,*
*I follow on through dangerous zones,*
*Cross dead men's bones and oceans stormy.*
*Some day I know she'll wait at last and*
*lock me fast in white embraces.*

*And down mysterious ways of love*
*We two shall move to fairy places.*

## Mary Ann

Mary Ann moved about more slowly these days. The little cottage seemed so silent. Francis had gone to the "big War" as the villagers spoke of it. Quinn had died two days before Christmas leaving Mary Ann to attend to all the chores. Perhaps it was just as well as it kept her mind busy and her days full. There wasn't an evening that she didn't open Francis' bedroom door and look upon the darkness to say good night to him. Sighing, she would walk to her room.

The postman was a favored visitor indeed these days. Mary Ann watched the road carefully, alert for the ring of his bicycle bell. Her white apron starched, and her hair tucked neatly under her muslin cap. She searched the lane eagerly to see if Mr. O'Neill had any news from Francis.

He was late this morning. He usually passed near onto ten o'clock. She picked some imaginary lint from her taffeta petticoat to occupy the time and spoke about to no one as was her habit of late.

"O'Neill, the devil take him—probably talking to the Cronins about the fair at Navan. Sure he's as bad a gabber as old Fergus, the station master. The news for miles always on his lips and he that eager to spread it thick!"

The bicycle turned the lane and its sharp bell brought her to attention.

"A letter it is for you, Mary Ann, and it's from himself," grinned O'Neill. She took the letter and carefully placed it into her apron pocket. Noting the eagerness to hear its contents so as to pass the news along with his next delivery, the postman leaned closer.

"Thank you Martin," Mary Ann acknowledged. "I'll be going in to sit and read the news now."

"That's two letters this month is it?" inquired O'Neill.

"Is it now?" Mary Ann raised her eyebrows in mock concern. "Be you counting for the record?" she inquired archly.

"My memory is my most precious possession," replied the postman grandly.

Mary Ann turned towards the cottage and before she reached the front step glanced over her shoulder to the proud man who now held his cap from his head in his usual salute of farewell.

"This one makes three; good day to you," said she smilingly and entered the cottage.

O'Neill placed his cap back on his head and pedaled briskly down the lane. He spent the rest of the day repeating to himself, "Sure she's wrong about three letters. Getting old she is poor soul. I count two and that's a fact be damned."

*And wondrous impudently sweet,*
*Half of him passion, half conceit,*
*The blackbird calls all down the street*

Many a Friday of each month Mary Ann went to Trim to put flowers on Patrick Ledwidge's grave. The headstone was simple; it included his name, birth, and death date.

Francis' mother was buried in the same plot also. The Sisters had seen to it all, using the money Francis had left them for that purpose. Patrick's second wife was buried with her first husband in Navan.

"So they are all in their proper places," Mary Ann said gazing at the tombstone. "Quiet they are; no talking here," she mused as she gazed over the cemetery sadly. "Are they gone forever or do they see each other in some other place? A heathen you are woman," she scolded herself. "Sure we don't remember our beginning! We just burst forth and there we were." She looked down on the simple grave. "It can't all end in silence now can it?"

"Good morning to you, Mary Ann." Pastor O'Connell stood quietly by the gate to the cemetery.

"Good morning to you, Pastor. My, I was so lost in my own thoughts, I didn't hear you."

"This is quite a little walk from Navan for you Mary Ann."

Mary Ann turned towards the gate wiping the perspiration from her forehead with a large white handkerchief. "Not too far Pastor, it's good to keep these old bones moving otherwise they'd dry up and leave me in the rocker."

The good pastor opened the gate allowing Mary Ann to join him on the dirt road. "I'll accompany you to Drogheda and the Navan market if I may," said the pastor.

"Thank you Father." The two walked along in silence. Then almost simultaneously each began a sentence. Laughingly the priest bowed and Mary Ann said, "Francis is fine, Pastor. He writes very often but says little of where he is or what is happening in the war with the Germans." The priest nodded. "He says he spoke with Lord Dunsany who is now Commander Dunsany and he seemed very happy at their reunion."

"I thought Lord Dunsany was in the same regiment as Francis," inquired the pastor.

"Oh he is Father, but from what I understand from Francis' letters, they do not meet very often."

"I can understand that as a regiment they would not meet very often. A regiment is a great number of men in various positions of command."

As they reached the Drogheda-Navan juncture the priest said quietly, "Please remember me to Francis, Mary Ann. Tell him I will remember him in my prayers."

"He'll be thanking you for that Pastor," Mary Ann said solemnly.

"It's a sad thing, that a man with such a great gift as he must take a gun into his hands. May he live to put it aside and take up the pen again. God bless you Mary Ann." He turned left down the lane to Drogheda and Mary Ann walked more slowly than before towards the cottage in Navan. The sun was setting in the vermilion sky. The crickets, tired from the heat of the July day, were silent. She didn't notice the blackbird sitting on the bough of a tree as she was so sadly occupied with thoughts of him so far away. When she passed, the bird flew high into the darkening sky and seemed for a time to follow the figure walking alone down the dirt road. One might have thought the bird was her only companion on that lonely journey home.

## The Blackbird

They looked like mummies wrapped in bandages. Some were led by others whose faces had the look of death. Each retreating soldier staring at seemingly nothing followed one another in pathetic disarray. They had come from the front lines and in a period between July and late September some three hundred and eighty thousand of them had been gassed or bayoneted by the Germans. They moved silently through Ledwidge's platoon down the road to Arras. At first Captain Payne had thought they were going back for a rest and that his command would replace them. In that surmise he was correct. But the Frenchmen who staggered or walked all morning past the British troops were the last remains of the forward French army, demoralized and mutinying. The soldiers gathered as many bottles of wine as they could and handed them to each passing French soldier. "Here take another," they said. The steady procession that swept over the meadow toward the main road seemed not to hear them and threw the bottles to the ground. Captain Payne blew his whistle and his men gathered in front of him.

"We shall proceed to our positions as outlined by your sergeant men. Those poor devils you see in retreat are heading for the rest they richly deserve. We shall take up against the Bosch in their place and give the Hun this day his due." Thank God Payne and the rest of the troops did not know the truth. The rest at the village of Messines had given the men some time to get ready for the battle they knew was inevitable. Adjusting their helmet straps and canteens, and placing their rifles against their shoulders they straggled down the road to battle. Perhaps victory would be theirs.

The day was humid and the rain came intermittently. The roads grew muddy. Ledwidge hadn't written Mary Ann for a fortnight. "I say the same things over and over—the weather—the latest Sergeant anecdote," he mused.

"Look smartly there Ledwidge," snapped the Sergeant. "We can't have you daydreaming now man."

"Now Sergeant, would you be spoiling my scheme to have us home by Christmas and maybe sooner if my plan to finish the Huns comes off?"

"Hear, hear," went up from the throats of the men marching more smartly upon hearing Ledwidge's response.

There arose in Francis a longing for home and the past. He recalled the trip to Ardonmore and then to the day he and Dunsany drove to Glendalough and talked of Ireland and her kings.

"I remember our conversation about our Ireland," he mused aloud as they bivouacked one evening on a sloping hill one mile from the front. He sank back into his trench and reminisced. "I was telling Dunsany why Ireland was our life blood. It was that our past and present were fused through those struggles that we will endure." He pressed his head against the cold wet earth. "Ellie, can you hear me? Are you close by? You know I half expect to look about and see you."

He smiled and saw a young boy wearing a green cap looking sadly back at a tender moving through the mist towards Cork. He saw again the gulls following the tender to shore. He longed to ride their wings. The stars were brilliant above him. He saw Mary Ann holding his gift of the seaconch. She was placing it to her ear. "I can hear the ocean right here in my very own parlor. Francis." He shifted his pack to the side of the trench that was dug not too deep. There was the cottage with the smokeless chimney and the door ajar with no one inside.

Ballynock rose through the night mist and he once again stood on her ramparts and surveyed his kingdom as Brian Boru.

He saw the salon of Dunsany at Ardenmore with its gilt chairs—and there were Yeats and O'Casey talking to him. And then he saw the smiling Nan standing outside his door trying to comfort a sad and desolate lad far from home. The scenes came and lingered with such vividness and with such sweeping emotion that he was totally lifted from his entrenchment.

"Be ready lads," whispered the Sergeant. "They'll be setting up their flares for us. Move in on the whistle." Hands pulled helmets tight, and packs and rifles were drawn close. The darkness exploded. Young bodies poised themselves for battle. The whistle sounded. Rockets lighted the sky with arches of white sulphur. Shells leaped from the smoking blackened mouths of cannons and the earth trembled in spasm of agony. The shouts of warriors filled the night.

The morning was silent. The guns had stopped and nothing moved in the meadow where but a few hours before hell had reigned.

*He shall not hear the bittern cry*
*in the wild sky, where he is lain,*
*Nor voices of the sweeter birds*
*Above the wailing of the rain…*

A bird, a blackbird, had wakened Francis and taken him to his place among the kings!

Printed in the United States
924000004B